Praise for
Lurking under the Surface:
Horror, Religion, and the Questions That Haunt Us

"Brandon Grafius combines biblical scholarship with a fanboy's love of horror to create a fun, fascinating book you won't be able to put down. I've never read a book quite like this."

—**Reza Aslan**, #1 *New York Times* best-selling author of
Zealot: The Life and Times of Jesus of Nazareth

"No matter how many times you've seen *Night of the Living Dead*, *The Thing*, or *Sinister*, this book will come to you as a revelation. Brandon Grafius not only knows horror—he understands the deeper questions dark fictions ask."

—**W. Scott Poole**, author of *Dark Carnivals:*
Modern Horror and the Origins of American
Empire and *Monsters in America*

"What a tasty book! It dives deep into what terrifies us, entertains us, and awakens the awe inside us. With a scholar's knowledge of both theology and every kind of horror movie, Grafius takes us on a tour of our soul with thought-provoking analysis, personal reflection from his own journey, and a healthy helping of humor."

—**Owen Egerton**, writer/director of *Mercy Black* and
author of *Hollow*

"Too often, believers approach horror movies as little more than the opportunity to reinforce cherished religious views. Grafius takes his subject much more seriously than that, exploring not only why these texts are important to believers, but how their importance lies precisely in that they raise the hard questions. If horror is the genre that takes religion at its word, Grafius takes horror the same way. Highly recommended."

—**Douglas E. Cowan**, professor of religious studies and social development studies at the University of Waterloo and author of *America's Dark Theologian: The Religious Imagination of Stephen King*

"This generous personal account demonstrates what horror fans have always known: that in exploring, and sometimes wallowing in, the darkest recesses of the human condition, we can find resilience, understanding, and hope."

—**Aislinn Clarke**, writer-director of *The Devil's Doorway* and lecturer in screenwriting and film, Queen's University, Belfast

"Grafius skillfully untangles the threads of belief, doubt, and the holy that give horror its enduring power, inviting us to reconsider both fear and faith. A book for horror fans, believers, skeptics, and everyone in between."

—**Rhiannon Graybill**, associate professor of religious studies at Rhodes College and author of *Texts after Terror: Rape, Sexual Violence, and the Hebrew Bible*

LURKING
UNDER THE
SURFACE

LURKING
UNDER THE
SURFACE

HORROR,
RELIGION,
AND THE
QUESTIONS
THAT HAUNT US

BRANDON R. GRAFIUS

Broadleaf Books

Minneapolis

LURKING UNDER THE SURFACE

Horror, Religion, and the Questions That Haunt Us

Cover image: AVTG/iStock
Cover design: 1517 Media

Print ISBN: 978-1-5064-8162-3
eBook ISBN: 978-1-5064-8163-0

CONTENTS

INTRODUCTION

BRING OUT YOUR DEAD!

PRECHAPTER VIEWING RECOMMENDATIONS

Night of the Living Dead (George Romero, 1968)

A WALK THROUGH THE GRAVEYARD

I live a few miles south of Michigan State University in a bucolic town that has deep roots as a farming community. There's a community garden right across the street from my house. You can walk through the garden's parking lot to the Hayhoe River Trail, winding along the banks of a slow-moving creek, which meanders through a rich forest of cedar and oak. But before it gets to the forest, the trail bends along the edge of Maple Grove Cemetery, a graveyard with stones that date to the 1800s. Even in the bright sunlight of a Michigan fall day, something makes me feel a little uneasy about walking around

---

the cemetery. I often find myself holding my breath for long stretches until I can get to the forest. Then, once I've crossed the bridge and left the cemetery behind, I can settle into my walk.

I don't think I appreciated this space enough until the pandemic hit, and daily masked walks became one of the few ways we were able to get out of our homes. I haven't taken it for granted since then. During my times in this space, my mind kept pondering all the ways the graveyard symbolizes the connections between life and death, the sacred and the terrifying. At first, these two experiences may seem like opposite ends of the spectrum. But the graveyard helps us to see that faith and fear are more closely connected than they appear.

Lurking under the Surface explores this connection between faith and horror, showing how horror can be a valuable—even important—conversation partner for the spiritual questions that animate so many of us. If we treat them both seriously, as I believe we should, horror movies and religion lead us through the same sets of questions. Both areas explore issues of justice, hope, and our relationship to the cosmos. And both offer us ways to make meaning out of the contradictory pieces of our world, a world that can seem so hopeful and yet so doom-laden, filled with sunshine but also much darkness.

Horror movies and television shows (and novels, myths, and folktales before there were movies!) have always helped us to process our fears and anxieties. Whether it's classic narratives that consider the consequences of stretching our knowledge further than it's safe to go, such as *Frankenstein* (1931), or more contemporary films that explore questions of racism and white guilt, such as *Get Out* (2017), horror is a window into the culture.

The same is true of religion. People's hopes and fears are often expressed in their religion and written down in their sacred books. I'm a biblical scholar by trade, so most of the examples in this book will come from the religious traditions I know best, but similar dynamics are at play in other religions as well. Both horror and religion wrestle with questions about the nature of life, our place in the universe, and what it means to be human. In *Lurking under the Surface*, I'll delve into some horror movies to see what they can tell us about religion and also what religion might be able to tell us about horror. And I'll explore how horror and faith can both support one another, leading us to refuse easy, facile answers to life's most important questions.

A warning to the reader: I'll do my best to stay away from spoilers, but it's impossible to talk about movies without having some! At the front of each chapter, I've included a short list of a few films that you might consider watching before reading the chapter, if you're interested. Any spoilers will be covered in those "prechapter viewing" film lists. Don't think of these viewing suggestions as assignments—I hope you'll enjoy each chapter whether you've seen any of the films under discussion or not. But if you're interested in exploring a little deeper, those films might help you appreciate the conversations even more.

In this book, we won't look away from the things that scare us. We'll walk through the graveyard—at night—and we'll notice how the frightening nocturnal graveyard is still a sacred space and the church in the daytime still holds potential horrors. We'll talk about hope and fear and how they are two reflections of the same image. We'll meditate on faith and doubt and how often these two ideas run side by side in horror films—and in religion.

As we walk together, my hope is that you'll start to think back on the horror movies you've loved—the ones that have kept you up at night over the years or still give you a rush of adrenaline when you think about them—and notice how important religious questions are to what makes those movies work. I'll keep coming back to these questions of meaning, especially: How do horror movies help us make sense of the world, in a way that scratches the same itch as religion? Looking at horror movies through this lens can enlighten us and help us see our favorite movies in new ways. And we'll walk through the graveyard together, because watching horror movies with someone else is always more fun.

"They're Coming to Get You"

George Romero's 1968 classic *Night of the Living Dead*, often considered the first modern horror film, starts off in a graveyard that looks a bit like the one across the street from me. Romero's cemetery is in Evans City, about thirty miles outside of Pittsburgh. Barbra and her brother, Johnny, have arrived there at twilight, right after the seasonal change to daylight saving time, which means that it's still uncannily light at 8:00 p.m. They've come to lay a small cross bearing the words "we still remember" at their father's grave. It's a religious symbol that isn't at all out of place among the graves and monuments. As Barbra kneels in front of the tombstone, Johnny fidgets awkwardly with his driving gloves.

"C'mon," he says to his sister, "I mean, praying's for church."

Barbra snips back, "I haven't seen you in church lately."

Johnny laughs, remembering a time when he had jumped out from behind a tree in the graveyard to scare his sister. She shudders, seemingly still troubled at the memory. For Barbra, this graveyard is a sacred space, a sanctuary where she prays over the memory of her father. But it is also a space of horror where she's always on edge and feels like the line between the living and the dead isn't quite solid enough for her liking. Just a few minutes after this scene ends, she'll have even more reason to fear the sacred space of the graveyard.

Even at their most placid, graveyards are eerie. They connect us with our ancestors and provide spaces for mourning and remembering, but they also offer a reminder of our eventual death. In a graveyard, it's easy to feel surrounded by that reminder, even when the sun is shining warmly and the birds call out from the nearby trees. The sacredness of the graveyard is entangled with this reminder of our own mortality, a disquieting thought that's not always possible to keep at bay.

That chilling feeling can quickly turn to horror, as happens dramatically in *Night of the Living Dead*. As Johnny mocks Barbra for her fear of the cemetery, with the famous line "They're coming to get you, Barbra!" one of the living dead shuffles toward her and attacks with little fanfare or warning. In the world of this film, the sacred turns quickly from the ordinary to the horrifying without so much as a squeal of tires. It happens as easily as "sacred" can become "scared" through a simple act of mistyping. The physical space of the graveyard is one of our first indications that the worlds of religion and horror are not, in fact, very far apart from each other. Often, they even share the same terrain.

In *Night of the Living Dead*, the cemetery becomes marked as sacred space by the act of Barbra and her brother bringing in a religious symbol and by Barbra's prayer. In the older churches of Europe and New England, this relationship is even closer—the graveyard is directly connected to the church, lying just outside the walls of the sanctuary but within the walled-in boundary of the church's property. The graveyard and the church occupy the same lot, likely cared for by the same groundskeeper. There, horror and the sacred intermingle.

Sometimes, it's only a matter of timing that determines whether the space of the graveyard is primarily sacred or horrifying. In the light of day, we may experience the graveyard as contemplative, perhaps melancholy, but the twinges of terror are pushed into the background of our thoughts. However, when the sun drops down and the songs of birds are replaced by the chirping of crickets, feelings of unease rise to the surface. Timing is everything. It's the difference between people who are on one side of the wall, sitting in the pews on a Sunday morning, and people who are on the other side, resting in the graveyard.

At other times, it's not the timing that transforms the sacred into the horrifying but an event. In the first *Phantasm* film (1979), young Mike watches a funeral from a distance through his binoculars, curious about the adult ritual he has been excluded from. But his curiosity turns to horror when he spies the undertaker, the series' iconic Tall Man, lifting the coffin back into his hearse effortlessly with just one hand. For the rest of the film, Mike understands that the graveyard is a place of danger and struggles to convince the rest of his community to recognize this as well.

The sanctuary is, in many ways, the graveyard's mirror image. It is sacred space that promises to protect and shelter all who enter. This is why gargoyles adorn the entranceways of many old European churches—these guardian monsters are supposed to ward off evil presences and keep the frightening realities of the world outside. The faithful can enter unharmed, under the watchful eye of the gargoyles. They mark the passageway into safe, sacred space.

But even in the supposedly safe confines of the church itself, timing may be a matter of life and death. In folk tales from many traditions, the church is not a safe place at night, as monsters take over and perform their own dark rituals. Finnish legends describe people who attempt to enter a church after dark only to be injured or struck ill as a result of their transgression. More directly, a Swedish folktale tells of an old woman who mistook the time and came to church too early one morning to be confronted by a ghostly minister preaching to an undead congregation. In these stories, even the sanctuary itself is only safe during the hours of daylight.[1]

Sometimes, the happenings of the secular world can also breach the walls of the sanctuary. The name of the worship space, *sanctuary*, indicates that it should be a safe refuge from the horrors of the world; too often, these horrors creep in. Sometimes, the problems we face, as individuals or as a society, are too large to forget about for the duration of the worship service. After horrific events like the terrorist attacks of 9/11, it's impossible for the sacred space to be a true sanctuary from the chaos outside because we continue to think about what these events mean for how we understand the world around us and the kind of God we are worshipping. The events are too powerful to keep out. And on a more literal level, churches struggled with how to maintain their identity as sanctuaries in the midst of the COVID-19 pandemic, when the traditional act of passing the peace could lead straight to the hospital. The coronavirus was no respecter of walls; the horrors of the world waltzed right into the church building. The monster may be sitting in the pew right next to us.

There can be other ways that horror enters sacred space. While the events of the world are frequently rushing the door, sometimes it's clergy who transform holy ground into a space of horror with their words. When pastors preach hatred against Jews, atheists, people of other ethnic groups, the LGBTQ community, or any other marginalized group, they've brought horror into the church. Then the monster isn't on the periphery but in the pulpit.

At other times, churches have intentionally transformed themselves into spaces of terror, attempting to use the power of horror to edge people on the road to "salvation." Starting in the 1970s and gaining popularity in the 1990s, many evangelical churches have sponsored Halloween "Hell Houses," a fundamentalist twist on the more traditional haunted house. Instead of being chased by zombies or attacked by masked employees wielding fake chain saws, spectators are treated to scenes of women obtaining abortions and dying at the hands of unscrupulous doctors or innocent young men seduced into the "homosexual lifestyle" only to find themselves burning in hell. It's as if Jonathan Edwards's famous sermon "Sinners in the Hands of an Angry God" has been brought to life and reimagined as a painting by Hieronymus Bosch.

For many people, these events are extremely distasteful, simply embodiments of the judgmental prejudices held by some religious communities. But for members of these faith groups, Hell Houses function just like horror movies do for the wider culture—they put Hell House participants in touch with their deep-seated fears and offer an opportunity to reflect on why those things are frightening.[2] It's another example of how the wall separating religion from horror is even thinner than the wall that divides the sanctuary from the graveyard.

ASKING THE QUESTIONS

Horror movies can make us mindful of the graveyard, a place that's unsettling, possibly deeply frightening if you visit at the wrong time, but where the sacred isn't too far away. In a horror film, the sacred might materialize in the form of a priest who can perform a successful exorcism only if he can first resolve his own faith crisis, like in *The Exorcist* (1973). Or it might appear in the symbols of a crucifix or a Bible, talismans that can be powerful weapons in the hands of a person whose faith is true. Even more often, we see religious questions being asked in a different way. Like religion, horror is preoccupied with questions of good and evil, asking where hope can be found in a world so full of darkness. Like religion, horror asks if there's justice in this life or, if not, maybe in the life to come. And like religion, horror asks us to think about our place in the universe, what it means to be human, and what meaning and purpose we might be able to find in this short life we've been given. The more you probe the walls between horror and religion, the more they start to collapse, leading us to realize we've been in the same space all along, whether it's the sanctuary or the graveyard. Overall, this shared space where horror and faith coexist uncomfortably is one in which we can try to envision what our life might mean.

Among people who study horror films, it's become a truism that these movies strike a chord with their culture. The ones that become big box office successes or are discussed in the *New York Times* usually reflect the anxieties of the day.[3] It's easy to see Cold War fears reflected in 1950s sci-fi and horror films, and scholar Robin Wood makes a compelling case that the countercultural horror films of the late 1960s and 1970s (including *Night of the Living Dead*) are reflections of a society that was struggling with questions of racial justice and the terror of the Vietnam War.[4]

And when people get anxious, horror is a bull market. We're drawn to horror entertainment when our anxieties rise: The first major boom was in the early 1930s, just as the Great Depression was getting underway; the second was the independent and drive-in movies of the late 1960s and early 1970s. Now we're finding ourselves in another one, which seems to have moved seamlessly from the economic and racial worries of the Obama era to the civil unrest America experienced during Trump's term in office—and, of course, into the COVID-19 pandemic. When people are apprehensive about social change, they turn to horror.

I'm well steeped in all these anxieties, and maybe as a result, I've been a horror fan almost my whole life. Since I was also pursuing religion as an academic discipline, I kept this part of myself locked up as a guilty pleasure for many years. But at some point, the connections became too strong for me to ignore, and it stopped making sense to keep these two parts of myself isolated in separate corners of the ring. Both horror and religion are about helping us make meaning out of our lives, positioning the disparate puzzle pieces that we get handed every day into a single picture. (Even if on some days it looks more like a Jackson Pollock than anything else.)

Throughout this book, I explore ways in which horror and religion are closely intertwined. Chapter 1 questions how watching horror movies can be a "moral" pastime and how staring into the darkness is both troubling and important. Chapter

2 employs the famous Psalm 23 to consider how we experience hope in our lives, using *The Walking Dead* as its main conversation partner. Chapter 3 looks at the power of faith in shaping our reality, while chapter 4 argues that both horror and religion help us think through our relationships with our own bodies. I think of chapters 5 and 6 as two halves of the same discussion, first exploring how the monster helps us define ourselves and then examining how desperately we want to be remembered after we've left this earth. Similarly, chapters 7 and 8 work as a paired discussion about the importance of fairness and justice to our religious journeys and to the world of horror. And finally, chapters 9 and 10 both look at doubts, with chapter 9 probing the reality that we don't always experience God as good (however much we may want to) and chapter 10 making an argument for doubt as both a crucial and unsettling aspect of our faith journey. By the end, I hope to have led you along a path that will help you see new depths in popular entertainment and also ponder your faith journey in a new and exciting way.

Much of this book was written during a global pandemic, a time when many people noted that real life began to feel like a horror movie. Depending on the day or the hour (and where we resided in the world), it might be an apocalyptic zombie movie where society is falling apart, we have to run to the garage to MacGyver some contraption together with duct tape that can help us defend ourselves, and there's no more toilet paper. It might be an invasion film where we're barricading ourselves up inside our homes to keep the dangerous killer from breaking through the windows. (Only in this case, the murderer is actually just our neighbor or a delivery person who is not wearing a mask.) Or it might be a found-footage horror film where something that seems close to reality is spliced together into a bunch of people running around in the woods and yelling, which usually ends in all of the main characters dying. *The Blair Zoom Meeting*, perhaps.

Even while we were living through these times, people kept streaming horror (at least when they could tear themselves away from the train wreck of *Tiger King*). Partially, it gave many of us something to do while we were at home with our families—watching a scary movie together is a great way to spend an evening. But even more than that, our favorite horror movies present a world where random, often terrifying, things happen, and we have to figure out what to do about it. The world of horror entertainment is less safe than our own, or so we like to think, but it is also more open to possibility, less confined, less straitjacketed by routine. When we feel our own world falling apart in ways large or small, it feels good to spend time in a world that isn't quite the same as what we're experiencing but has enough overlap that we can see the connections. The times may be anxious, but sharing that anxiety with others—either those we're sitting with on the couch or those characters we're watching on the screen—can make the dread a little more manageable.

Horror helps us perceive the world around us in new ways; it also shows us things that our religious traditions have been pointing out all along that we haven't wanted to acknowledge. Watching and thinking about horror can guide us through the graveyard with the same purpose as religion: helping us see the world as a bigger place than we imagined and experience it in all of its wonderful, terrifying messiness.

I

WE CAN'T LOOK AWAY

PRECHAPTER VIEWING RECOMMENDATIONS

Something Wicked This Way Comes (Jack Clayton, 1983)
The Ring (Gore Verbinski, 2002)
Sinister (Scott Derrickson, 2012)

I 've lived most of my life with one foot in the world of horror and one in the world of the church. How can these two elements coexist? It seems like a paradox: religion is a pursuit of the grace and love that the faithful believe lies at the heart of the universe, while horror fixates on the darkness and cruelty that lie just below the world's surface. But as the introduction explores, we don't have to view these two modes of thinking—horror and religion—as opposite ends of a straight line. It's more like a circle, with the two ends wrapping around to meet each other.

This chapter explores one of the ways that horror and religion meet, in their mutual assertion that the entire experience of life matters. Both horror and religion tell us that we have to pay attention to all of it. That means enjoying the good parts while also looking evil square in the face without blinking. It's easy to smile at what makes us happy in life, whether it's a sunlit walk or a sermon that tells us God loves us. It's harder to gaze at what's painful and ugly, and both horror and religion understand that. But they also both realize how important it is to do so. If we only behold the sunshine, we miss so much of life.

So in this chapter, I'd like to tell you some stories about how I started looking and why I still can't look away, as well as how religion and horror both acknowledge how uncomfortable this can be but encourage us to keep looking anyway.

SEARCHING FOR SERIOUS HORROR

I have clear memories of watching *Scooby-Doo* on TV every afternoon when I was a kid. Back then, long before the ubiquitous streaming of today, we had to watch whatever the networks let us watch. This made each afternoon at 3:30 like unwrapping a Christmas present. Sometimes it was a disappointment—even as a preschooler, I knew that the episodes with Scrappy-Doo sucked. I've come to think of him as Saturday morning's biggest party-crasher, breaking up the Mystery Gang. And sometimes it was a little much for my three-year-old brain to handle—when the episode with the witch doctor Mamba Wamba came on, I changed the channel quickly. (The whole image is deeply offensive; horror has always explored our fear of what's different, which means the history of the genre is replete with painful stereotypes.) But mostly, the cartoon offered a gripping world of hidden passages, mysterious fog, and dangerous monsters. Each day when my dad got home from work, I would run to the front door to tell him who the bad guy had been on *Scooby-Doo* because I was sure he just had to know what he'd missed. It didn't matter that every episode ended with Old Man Withers in a rubber mask.

At least, it didn't matter for a while. *Scooby-Doo* was my gateway substance into horror, but it wasn't long before I needed something else. My next step came packaged in a white clamshell case with the Disney logo on top of it. This should have marked the movie inside as safe entertainment, something that parents could set their child in front of without worry for an hour and a half. But this VHS tape from the library was *Something Wicked This Way Comes* (1983), a Jack Clayton–directed Disney adaptation of Ray Bradbury's supremely creepy novel.

In *Something Wicked This Way Comes*, there were no rubber masks. There was only the terrifying Mr. Dark (played with deliciously evil relish by Jonathan Pryce), the ringmaster of a traveling carnival who may or may not have been the devil himself. He certainly had the power to know the secret desires of everybody in town and to make them come true. But when people accepted these gifts, they found themselves trapped in

Mr. Dark's carnival, a permanent part of the traveling show. The most tempting attraction in the carnival was the carousel; people would come after dark, and it would run backward, making them younger with each revolution. For the children in town, it could fulfill their dreams of growing older, instantly turning them into adults who would be taken seriously and could "learn what grown-ups do behind locked doors," in the enticingly ominous words of Mr. Dark. This movie offered a peek behind the curtains of life in a way that felt exhilarating to a six-year-old, so I watched it again and again.

I went through the same trajectory with books. The Hardy Boys were my literary Scooby-Doo, and as soon as I could read chapter books, I tore through them, often two or more per week, impatient to learn what the secret of the old mill was. But at the end of each book, the plot was revealed to have been disturbingly facile. There was never any real danger, so I walked away from the book feeling both disappointed and insulted. And then I ran down to the library to grab another one because *this* one would actually be good, I was certain.

After a few months of playing the role of Charlie Brown while the Hardy Boys yanked the football away from me, I asked my librarian for help. "I want a book where people die" was all I could think to tell her, not something like the Hardy Boys, where nothing had real consequences and order was almost immediately restored. Looking back on the request, I've got to imagine she was completely baffled by this rather odd and morbid kid, but she did her best and handed me a copy of *Tuck Everlasting*, about a family that has a fountain of youth in the woods behind their house. It wasn't quite what I was looking for, but I'm grateful for her effort to this day. Instead, I found the high fantasy of Lloyd Alexander's The Chronicles of Prydain, followed by some Tolkien. But it was when I discovered Edgar Allan Poe that my reading really took off.

The darkness tapped into something in me, though I wasn't sure why. I was a pretty happy child, from a loving family; what drew me to *Something Wicked This Way Comes* and Poe? And why, week after week, do so many of us keep going to the theaters or streaming movies that delve into the darkest corners of the world? Why do we keep looking?

THINK ON THESE THINGS

I often encounter people who know of my background in biblical studies and want to discuss how Christians can watch horror films with a clear conscience. Christians are supposed to be pursuing a virtuous life, they feel, not subjecting themselves to violent images and nastiness. I understand this question and take it seriously; it's one I struggle with as well. One of my mother's favorite Bible verses is from Paul's letter to the Philippians, where he writes, "whatever is true, whatever is honorable, whatever is just, whatever is pure, whatever is pleasing, whatever is commendable, if there is any excellence and if there is anything worthy of praise, think about these things" (4:8). Think about the good in life, and don't spend your time dwelling on the awfulness. That would seem to rule out enjoying horror movies, right?

This has been the line taken by some Christian groups for as long as there have been movies. In the 1930s, as the film industry was becoming a major business, Hollywood developed the Hays Code as a way to appease the moral concerns of the Catholic Church. Among other items, the Hays Code allowed for little to no direct talk of sexuality, and depictions of violence were tightly constrained. If a man was going to be shot, filmmakers were discouraged from presenting both the shooter and the victim in the same frame without an intervening edit, as a way to limit the impact of the violence.[1] Even more than questions of explicit sex and violence, the Hays Code was concerned with the general morality of movies. Prostitution or premarital sex could be discussed only in oblique ways. If you've seen the 1934 classic *It Happened One Night*, starring Clark Gable and Claudette Colbert, you'll probably remember the famous scene where the two protagonists end up having to share a room in a bed and breakfast. Clark Gable sanctimoniously hangs up a bedsheet to divide the room in half and proclaims it "The Wall of Jericho," to make sure the audience knew that nothing untoward was going on between these characters. Even marital sex could only be hinted at: after the two characters get married, the sounds of an off-key children's trumpet ring out, and the film ends on a close-up of the hanging bedsheet falling to the ground. Just like in Joshua, the walls have come tumbling down.

Most importantly, if someone did something bad in a movie, they had to be punished by the end. The Hays Code held throughout the 1940s and the 1950s until it gradually unraveled in the 1960s, to be replaced by the Motion Picture Association of America's (MPAA) rating system. It started off with just G and R, but has gradually expanded into what we know today, with ratings of G, PG, PG-13, and R (and, very infrequently, NC-17).

Ratings aren't the only ways that religious groups have pushed back against content they deem offensive. Catholic groups organized nationwide protests against *The Exorcist* in 1973, and a family-values group in Wisconsin held rallies against the holiday slasher *Silent Night, Deadly Night* (1984) after the film's producer made the mistake of running ads featuring an ax-wielding Santa Claus during a Green Bay Packers' football game. This campaign spread to other cities, and was successful enough that *Silent Night, Deadly Night* was pulled from theaters before it made it to the West Coast. (Then again, maybe it just wasn't a very good movie.)

Even today, you don't have to search long on Google to find a slew of bloggers who argue that watching horror movies is bad for Christians' souls. I understand the argument, but it's also incomplete.

The first part of my response is to ask (usually just to myself, because I'm generally a polite person) if the people making this argument have ever read the Bible. It's full of horrible things that people do to one another, frequently with God's approval. The Hebrew Bible/Old Testament features wars and devastation, torture and dismemberment, sexual violence, and lots of general unpleasantness, often described in graphic detail. While much of the New Testament is a calmer place, Jesus occasionally loses his cool and talks about people being thrown into outer darkness, with wailing and gnashing of teeth. And there's the crucifixion and all the brutality surrounding it, which someone might be able to make into a great horror film if Mel Gibson hadn't already done it. If that weren't enough, the New Testament ends in a flurry of violence in Revelation, culminating in wicked people being thrown into a lake of fire. These events might constitute the "whatever is true" that Paul was thinking about, but it's harder to describe them as honorable, just, pure, pleasing, or commendable. The Bible itself is full of as much ugliness as any number of contemporary horror movies.

But this still doesn't address the basic question, which argues that exposing yourself to questionable content can be dangerous. Both the Bible and horror films suggest that watching can lead to negative consequences, though perhaps in slightly different ways. For example, in the Bible, King David gets himself into a world of trouble when he pauses in his evening stroll along the palace roof to peep at the bathing beauty Bathsheba. After these few moments of watching her, David loses all sense of responsibility. He has Bathsheba brought to the palace to have sex with him, even though he knows she is a married woman, and then orchestrates the death of her husband through treachery on the battlefield. (You can read all the lurid details in 2 Samuel 11.) This story ends with a curse being laid on the House of David, which will eventually result in the kingdom of Israel being split in two by civil war. All initiated because David couldn't stop himself from looking. Jesus warns his followers, "If your eye causes you to stumble, tear it out" (Matthew 18:9; Mark 9:47). Looking is dangerous, so perhaps it's better not to look.

Horror movies have long taken seriously the idea that looking is dangerous. Frequently in horror movies, there is no safe distance from which to watch. We could easily trace this motif all the way back to Luis Buñuel's surrealist 1929 silent film, *Un Chien Andalou* (An Andalusian Dog). The film opens with a woman staring into the camera; without warning, she produces a razor blade and slices her eyeball open. (It was actually a sheep's eyeball, filmed with a trick of perspective.) For this spectator, watching a film is like having her eyeball sliced open. In case this metaphor is too subtle, jump ahead to Michael Powell's notorious 1960 film, *Peeping Tom*, referred to by the ghostface killer of *Scream 4* as history's first slasher film. Beating *Psycho* (1960) to the punch by a few months, *Peeping Tom* features a photographer who spends his evenings murdering sex workers and other women he encounters. His method is a knife embedded in one of the legs of his camera tripod, which allows him to film the women as they are being murdered. As the audience, we watch through the camera's eye as the women scream while they are being stabbed. In some way, watching the movie is like being killers ourselves.

In the last couple of decades, two popular films have centered on the very act of watching horror movies and explored how dangerous this act can be. In the world of horror, there are always taboo acts, like sex and drinking in the *Friday the 13th* franchise or visiting a grave that shouldn't be disturbed. Violating these taboos is a risky endeavor. In *The Ring* and *Sinister*, the taboo act is watching a horror movie.

The Ring (and here I speak of the 2002 American remake, which is based on the 1998 Japanese sensation *Ringu*) features a spooky videotape, full of surrealist images of dead horses on the seashore, ominous-looking empty chairs, and mirrors whose reflections can't be tracked to any object in the real world. For the characters in the film, the mere act of watching this disturbing video starts the countdown to their death. Each viewer receives a phone call immediately afterward. The voice on the other end of the phone tells them, "Seven days," which is how much time they have left to live. Sending the call to voice mail doesn't let anyone off the hook, as one of the characters discovers.

After some determined investigating, the film's protagonists discover that this tape was created (through unspecified supernatural means) by a ghost named Samarra who was horribly mistreated as a child and murdered by her mother. The tape lives on as an embodiment of her rage. Once someone has seen the tape, there's only one way to avoid a death sentence from the ghostly Samarra: make a copy and show it to someone else. This way, the record of Samarra's anguish lives on and spreads from person to person. Viewing is dangerous, *The Ring* tells us, but transferring the terror to someone else wards off your own horrible fate.[2]

Perhaps even less hopeful about the nature of looking is the 2012 film *Sinister*. It's a deeply chilling film and probably the darkest that I'll analyze in this book. The story centers on a true-crime writer named Ellison (Ethan Hawke) who has been struggling to produce a follow-up to his first hit. He convinces his family that moving to a new home in a different community will help kick-start his writing; what he doesn't tell them is that the family who lived in the house previously was murdered and their youngest child never found. This unsolved murder is to be the subject of Ellison's next book. (In another illustration of how the morals of Christianity and horror films overlap, keeping secrets from your family is usually not a good idea.) Ellison's research is galvanized when he finds a box of Super 8 films in the house's attic; one of the movies is a grainy recording of the family being hanged in a tree in the backyard. What Ellison will figure out by the end of the film—too late to do him any good—is that his own fate was sealed as soon as he watched this movie.

Ellison's research leads him to uncover a grisly pattern in which many people before him had discovered a box of Super 8 tapes in their attic. The culprit behind all of this is a fictionalized, vaguely Mesopotamian demon named Bughuul; in the mythology of the movie, he is the demon of images. He moves through the videos that are planted in these houses. The household is marked once someone in the family sees the movie of its previous residents' demise. This allows Bughuul to enter the house and claim the family's youngest child for his own, which is why the youngest child is never found at the scene of the murders. At *Sinister*'s conclusion, this pattern repeats itself, as Ellison's youngest daughter dispatches her family with an ax. After she passes into the Super 8 movie playing in the background, joining Bughuul, the demon stares beyond the confines of the screen, fixing his gaze on the audience. He knows that we, too, have been watching.

In both *The Ring* and *Sinister*, watching horror films is what marks the characters for death. Whether it's the supernatural surrealism of *The Ring* or the Super 8 snuff films of *Sinister*, both films depict characters who die because of what they've watched. And in both cases, looking is contagious—in *The Ring*, sharing what you've seen is the only way to stave off your death, and in *Sinister*, one family's death produces the horror film that will condemn the next. It's a vicious cycle of watching.

I wonder if this focus on the guilt of watching explains why these two films scared me as much as any I've watched as a grown-up. In the case of *The Ring*, there hadn't been much great horror in the theaters for a while, as the 1990s were kind of a drought. Things were starting to pick up at the tail end of the decade with *The Sixth Sense* and *The Blair Witch Project* (both 1999), but in general, the decade was a horror wasteland. (Before the Obama years, critics had often noted that horror boomed under Republican presidents and waned under Democrats. In a nutshell, I'd propose that Americans are drawn to the Manichean moralism of Republican leaders in times of anxiety; as we saw in the introduction, anxiety is also what drives horror.) So when I went to see *The Ring* at a late-night weekend showing at a multiplex in California, I didn't expect something so eerie, something that dug under my skin so deeply. It was only rated PG-13, after all. But when I went home that night, I couldn't sleep—I kept thinking of Samarra climbing out of the television set.

The experience was slightly different with *Sinister*. It was ten years later, when I was a father and a PhD student. I had a big paper due on Monday, and my then-wife had taken the kids off on a weekend camping trip, both to give me some space to focus and to keep my stress from infecting her. Saturday evening, after a long day of writing and researching, I decided to unwind with a horror film. The hallways of my house did not feel safe that night, and I'm sure part of it was feeling my own guilt at having watched what just unfolded on the screen.

Both movies conform to the conservative Christian viewpoint that suggests watching horror films is dangerous. *Yes*, they say, *it is*. But *The Ring* and *Sinister* also understand a truth that those Christians often gloss over, although the Bible seems to know it well: we can't always look away. Whether because we're products of our culture and violence is all around us or perhaps because there's something damaged in us that's drawn to this violence, we can't look away. Perhaps more to the point, we don't look away because horror shows us something about what it means to be human. This is the same reason that the Bible is filled with tales of murder, deceit, and violence: this undercurrent is part of our nature as human beings, as we relate to other human beings in ways that are not always positive. According to the story of the Bible, it took a single generation for murder to become part of the human condition; violence has been with us ever since. We don't look away because to do so would deny part of what it means to be human.

2

THE VALLEY OF THE SHADOW

PRECHAPTER VIEWING RECOMMENDATIONS

The Walking Dead (even just the first two or
three episodes of season 1)
A Quiet Place (John Krasinski, 2018)
The Thing (John Carpenter, 1982)

In all of the Bible, there are few passages as beloved as Psalm 23. In the King James Version (KJV), the version many of us know by heart, the poem begins:

> The LORD is my shepherd; I shall not want.
> He maketh me to lie down in green pastures: he leadeth
> me beside the still waters.

It's a beautiful image of comfort and consolation. It's easy to imagine the lush grass against our skin, feel the sunshine on our faces, and hear the soft breeze rustling along the gentle stream. It presents us with a vision of having all of our needs met, of being cared for and looked after. There are no worries in these images, no need to look over our shoulder or fear what tomorrow may bring. These comforting thoughts are why this poem is frequently read at funerals, as a reminder to the congregation that the dearly departed is being cared for in a good place.

But in the midst of these pastoral images, there are some dark corners. If we read the psalm closely, part of its message to us is about the hard work it can take to get to hope. Green pastures might be the destination, but the poem is also about the harrowing journey on the way there. While most people don't think of horror movies while they're reading Psalm 23, this idea of the difficult struggle on the journey toward hope is something the two of them have in common. In this chapter, we will walk together through the valley of the shadow.

THREE JOURNEYS

Along with its plaintive images, Psalm 23 is a poem of journeys, with a subtle tension between motion and rest. In the imagery quoted previously, we see both stillness and motion: the psalmist rests by lying down in the green pastures but also walks by the still waters. Through the course of the brief poem, which is only six verses long, the psalmist goes on a total of three journeys (with a fourth that might be implied) before finally arriving at a banquet table. Then the writer is granted rest in the house of the Lord. Even though the three journeys are described only briefly, each has its own unique characteristics.

The first journey is the one beside the still waters. We might imagine a languid, strolling afternoon walk. Think of a Sunday afternoon, maybe with your family or loved ones, soaking in the peace of a warm day. Maybe there's a group of ducks floating along the pond next to you or a cardinal singing an inviting song. All is right with the world, and you are centered within yourself. This first journey is a peaceful one.

The second journey is phrased with equal optimism, but it's a longer trek, more fraught with peril. "He leadeth me in the paths of righteousness," the psalmist continues, "for his name's sake." The image is less concrete than a walk beside still waters, harder to visualize and feel. And it seems more of a lifelong journey than a stroll on a Sunday afternoon. The path to the still waters might be one we'll take many times in our lives, but the paths of righteousness go on forever, and we keep walking them. The tone of this journey is more ambiguous than it first appears. While the paths of righteousness might call to mind a blessed, prosperous journey where everything goes right, these could also be the paths that Mahatma Gandhi walked, or Martin Luther King Jr., or any other number of modern-day martyrs. Paths of righteousness aren't always easy, and walking them isn't necessarily comforting or joyful. It's not a Sunday stroll by the pond.

By the third journey, there's no doubt that we're a long way from a peaceful afternoon ramble. "Yea, thou I walk through the valley of the shadow of death," the psalmist writes, "I will fear no evil." This valley of *tzalmavet*, which might be more literally translated as "deep darkness," is poetically rendered as the valley "of the shadow of death" in the King James Version. It's not simply "the valley of death," which would indicate a physically dangerous or threatening place; it's a valley where death looms over everything, where death stretches out and envelops us. Shadows are larger than the object that creates them—they lengthen and surround everything they touch. In this valley, death casts a shadow large enough to swallow the psalmist.

But even while on this journey through terrifying shadow, the psalmist "will fear no evil." This sounds comforting, right? In some ways, it is. But "will" is an interesting word. It can mean we're convinced that something will or will not happen. We might say, "The sun will rise tomorrow morning," because we know beyond a doubt this is true. Maybe the psalmist is using "will" in this way: "I will not be afraid, as surely as the sun will rise." But we can also use "will" to indicate something we're resolved to do, even though we know it's going to be a struggle. "I will finish my homework by bedtime." "I will make sure to get this report done for my boss." "I will become a better spouse." These expressions of "will" are more tenuous; they're hopeful, yes, but they also indicate the speaker's acknowledgment that this is going to be a tough task. Not being afraid as we walk through the valley of the shadow of death might be more of this kind of "will": it's something we want desperately to convince ourselves we can do, even if it means we'll have to dig deep into ourselves to accomplish it.

There's a hidden fourth journey in Psalm 23, one that doesn't come through very well in most English translations. "Surely goodness and mercy shall follow me all the days of my life," the psalmist says with gratitude, before reaching the journey's end in the house of the Lord. As psalms scholar Clinton McCann points out, the Hebrew word that gets translated here as "follow," *radaph*, usually has other connotations.[1] When this word gets used, it doesn't signify following in a benign, supportive sense. Usually, it means "pursue" or "chase," or even "hunt down." It's the verb that describes Pharaoh chasing the Israelites after they've fled from Egypt in Exodus and what the armies of Joshua do to the Canaanites after they've been victorious in battle. It's frequently used in military contexts when there's hostility between the two parties. The party running ahead isn't being kindly followed so much as they are running for their lives. But in Psalm 23, the psalmist is being hunted down by goodness and mercy. It's a surprising blend of images, an incongruity that gets at both the hope and the fear that this psalm has explored.

HOPE AND FEAR AS REFLECTIONS

One thing a close reading of Psalm 23 shows us is that hope and fear are deeply related. I would be tempted to say that fear is hope's reflection, but perhaps it's better to see them as reflections of each other. If we don't read Psalm 23 closely, it's easy to gloss over the fear that underlies this poem. In the same way, if we don't pay attention to horror movies, we risk missing the hope that they hold on to. Since horror movies have fear right on the surface, that's often the only thing we see. But they also, perhaps surprisingly, speak to our hopes as well. In a world filled with horror, hope is a necessary thing to cling to. Often, we even find ways to make our visions of hope expand to match the overwhelming challenges we are up against.

For many horror films, particularly ones from the 1950s and earlier, hope is obvious and overt. Film critic Robin Wood has identified what he refers to as the "basic formula" for horror films: Normalcy is threatened by the monster. After this threat emerges, people band together to fight its intrusion into their lives, and the world is restored to normal.[2] Dracula comes from Transylvania to suck blood, but the people unite to defeat him (*Dracula*, 1931). Unsuspecting archaeologists awaken the mummy from his Egyptian tomb, but by the end of the movie, the mummy has been subdued, with some divine intervention from the goddess Isis (*The Mummy*, 1932).

The unspoken hope in these films is that the "normal" world is a safe and nourishing place. And even when it's threatened, we can overcome the menace and return to this orderly, familiar world. Monsters can be beaten. And if they come back (e.g., in a sequel), we know we'll be able to conquer them again. Horror movies that work like this reinforce our trust in the basic structures of our world, implying that we're strong enough to overcome any trouble that may assail us from the outside, whether it's an invading army, a crashed economy, or a terrible virus. We can hold on to the hope that the monstrous forces aligned against us will be vanquished in the end, and life will go back to normal.

But what if it's not that simple?

For many viewers, AMC's long-running zombie series *The Walking Dead* is unrelentingly bleak, with the remnants of humanity continually fighting for survival against ever-increasing odds. Viewers have come to know that none of their favorite characters are safe from a permanent exit from the show. But as biblical scholar Kelly J. Murphy has discussed, hope is one of the major themes in *The Walking Dead* as well as in the original comics on which the TV series was based. She writes, "In *The Walking Dead*, the zombie apocalypse is rooted, ultimately, in the hope that *humanity* might turn to good, to rebuilding, to restoring—even in the face of evil."[3] And indeed, a close inspection of the series reveals that hope is the driving force behind most of the characters' actions. They have been thrown into one of the most awful situations imaginable, but they understand they need to find something to hope for in order to keep moving forward. Amazingly, though many of the characters experience their object of hope dissolving or realize it was an illusion all along, they find something new to hope for rather than give up.

When Sheriff Rick Grimes first wakes up from a coma, he finds that the world has changed dramatically while he's been asleep. The dead have come to life, and most of society's dependable structures have fallen apart. He hopes that his wife and son might, somehow, have survived and that they are waiting for him so they can navigate this terrifying new world together. Unsure what steps to take, he happens to meet Morgan Jones, another survivor who is also holding out hope for himself and his son. In a poignant vein, Morgan is aware on some level that he needs to let go of his lingering hope for his wife. She's been turned into one of the walking dead, and comes to Morgan's house every night, but Morgan can't bring himself to shoot her. Hope dies hard. Morgan is not ready to leave yet, but he tells Rick of a band of survivors who headed down to Atlanta, and the two men promise to stay in touch. With little besides a shotgun and hope, Rick heads off to Atlanta in search of his family. It's one of many journeys that Rick, along with all of the characters in the series, will take through the valley of the shadow of death.

Rick rejoins his family (with much exciting melodrama along the way), who have banded together with some survivors outside of Atlanta. Cities are no longer habitable, having been overrun by the "walkers." The refugees are doing the best they can to rebuild their lives in the midst of a broken world, so they task themselves with finding something to hope for. At first, their hope is that there are survivors holing up in the Centers for Disease Control and Prevention headquarters in Atlanta. When this proves to be an illusion, they do not give up but successfully pivot, moving on to the next hope. It's what keeps them going from episode to episode, season to season.

The blockbuster horror-thriller *A Quiet Place* (2018) is similarly focused on the hope that can remain in the midst of everything falling apart. In that film, Earth has been besieged by hostile aliens who swoop down seemingly out of nowhere to grab their prey and carry them away. The aliens are effective enough as predators that only small groups of humans remain, though the film's focus on a single family gives us little insight as to how many survivors there might be. The key to survival is silence; unlike predators we're more familiar with, the aliens don't hunt by sight or smell but by sound. The Abbott family has adapted to a life of nearly complete silence, speaking in whispers inside their soundproof basement and using American Sign Language when outside.

But in the bleakness of these surroundings, they're doing what they can to be hopeful. Daughter Regan is deaf, and father Lee (writer-director John Krasinski, heavily bearded and serious) spends most of his free time learning about her hearing aid and working through plans to improve it. Even in the most dire scenarios, he holds on to the hope of making his daughter's life better.

In many twenty-first-century horror films with apocalyptic scenarios, hope is the driving force. This might be most obvious in *World War Z* (2013), where the main goal is finding a cure for a rapidly spreading zombie pandemic. We also see the question of hope arise just as strongly in director Susanne Bier's *Bird Box* (2018), with Malorie's (Sandra Bullock) determination to ensure the survival of her children and find a safe place for them to grow up. One of the film's main questions is what life looks like when survival itself is the only hope we can cling to and how important it is for us to find something else to live for. Frequently, apocalyptic television shows and films such as *The Walking Dead* and *A Quiet Place* utilize their apocalyptic scenarios to ask one key question: If everything about your life changed, what is the hope you would hold on to?

HOPE WHEN THERE'S NO HOPE

Of course, many horror narratives do not offer these kinds of possibilities for hope. In *Night of the Living Dead* (1968), the film's protagonist, Ben, has survived the night in the face of both the undead horde and the infighting among his fellow humans. He believes he's been saved when he sees an armed posse coming through the field to clear out the dead, only to be mistaken for one of the zombies and shot. Because Ben is African American, this bleak ending has been interpreted as a description of race relations in America in the 1960s (though George Romero has stated that the actor's race had nothing to do with him being cast as Ben) or as an allegory for America's hopeless involvement with the Vietnam War. Others have considered the finale more broadly as a critique of the patriarchal family unit in modern American culture. It's hard to find hope in the film's final images of our protagonist's dead body being thrown onto the pyre of zombie corpses. The other entries in Romero's *Dead* series don't leave the viewer with much more hope, either. In a similar vein, writer-director Jordan Peele has discussed his original ending of *Get Out* (2017): when the police show up, rather than helping protagonist Chris, they shoot him for the murders he had committed in self-defense. After Donald Trump's election, Peele felt like ending the film with an

African American being shot was too cruel to audiences, so he changed it.[4]

Another famously bleak conclusion is John Carpenter's 1982 classic *The Thing*. Loosely based on the 1951 sci-fi film *The Thing from Another World*, Carpenter's film follows a band of scientists at an Antarctic research station as they unearth an alien life form that is able to replicate its victims. Soon, none of the researchers knows who is a survivor and who is a monstrous presence in disguise. The film ends with the two final survivors sitting by the burning remains of the research station, drinking their last bottle of whiskey, knowing that the wintry elements will take them before long. It's unclear whether the research crew has succeeded in killing the Thing, hence stopping it from spreading to the rest of the world, or if this extraterrestrial invader is just beginning its conquest. This is downbeat stuff.

Viewers who watch a lot of horror could provide many more examples. There are the ghosts who spread like an epidemic in the Japanese film *Ju-On: The Grudge* (2002), targeting anyone who comes into their house and gradually consuming the entire city (if not the world). There's *Cabin Fever* (2002), in which a flesh-eating virus shows no sign of slowing down by the film's end. Or the climate change horror *The Last Winter* (2006), with its final image of a melted permafrost flooding a small town above the Arctic Circle, as the main character stands knee deep in water and warm rain. These are only a few examples to demonstrate that horror is one of the very few Western, mainstream genres where a happy ending isn't guaranteed.

What do movies like these have to do with hope?

Think of a piece of construction paper. Now imagine cutting a hole out of the center and throwing that piece away. That circle is gone from the piece of paper, but you can still see the shape of it by its absence. You can tell what used to be there. I would suggest that in these films and countless others, you can still sense the shape of hope by the bleak absence of hope for the films' characters. These movies take the complete lack of hope and ask us to think about what shape hope might take in our own lives.

Hope and fear are intertwined with each other and impossible to separate.

Psalm 23 is, in many ways, a poem about hope. It's about the hope of comfort, the hope of rest, the hope of having our needs met. It speaks to being content with having enough to continue, of getting to a place inside our heads where "we shall not want," and we can trust that our lives will work out. But it's also a poem about the valleys of the shadow that we sometimes have to walk through to get to that security. It's a poem that knows that getting to the good life doesn't come easily and that it might be a long journey to get there. On our way, we have to face our fears and try to keep holding on to hope.

In the same way, a show like *The Walking Dead* is about the journey from fear into hope. The show's characters find themselves in terrifying situations, where any breath could be their last. In this climate of constant fear, every step takes them deeper into the valley of the shadow. When you're walking through the valley, the only way out is to put one foot in front of the other. Horror teaches us that the way to survive is to constantly remind ourselves of the hope we're heading toward. And if that hope disappears, then we must find another idea to hope for.

THE FEAR BELOW THE SURFACE

The Walking Dead demonstrates another key truth about horror films and television shows, or at least good ones, and how they relate to hope and fear. There's always a fear on the surface—in this case, the specter of being ingested by a horde of snack-crazed zombies. But there's also a fear below the surface, and it's this deeper terror that usually connects most directly to the lives of the viewers. *The Walking Dead* speaks to our fears that our society is not built on a firm foundation and could come crashing down around us at any time. It's a fear that feels particularly acute in the twenty-first century, as we've increasingly lost trust in the institutions and authorities that have kept our society running—and even more so in the ravaged landscape that COVID-19 left in its wake.

It's a truism that every society on earth, for at least as long as we have records of human culture, has thought their generation might be the last. For example, apocalyptic movements arose after the death of Jesus, their adherents convinced that he would return before their generation died off and that this would usher in the end of the world as they knew it. Nearly a thousand years later, some people were convinced that the year 1000 was somehow a magical endpoint, and that the world would disappear in the blink of an eye at the stroke of midnight.[5]

We saw this again in the lead-up to 2000, when the apocalypse had a technophobic slant with fears of the impending Y2K computer disaster. And there have always been people who believed that whatever calamity had most recently befallen the world was a sure sign of God's imminent and final wrath.

Most of us don't buy into simplistic explanations of divine causes for current events. But we still have deep anxieties about the sustainability of the lives we lead and whether the social structures that allow for those lives are robust enough to survive the present moment. Sometimes, those fears come closer to the surface, especially in times of war, economic devastation, and widespread sickness. These are the seasons when the genre of apocalyptic horror rises to the surface. Perhaps they're also the times when we need it most.

Apocalyptic movies had a major moment in the 1970s, which was when big-budget disaster flicks like *Airport*, *The Poseidon Adventure*, and *The Towering Inferno* made huge profits by depicting devastating calamities on the big screen.[6] It was also a time when America was reeling from the Vietnam War and its aftereffects, the Cold War was continuing unabated, and the nation's economic outlook was uncertain at best. Every visit to the gas station was a reminder of the precarious state of the world. Around the same time, George Romero's *Dead* movies raised the bar for what independent films could be and what kind of profits they could generate.

At the turn of the twenty-first century, apocalyptic film and television came roaring back, this time more explicitly packaged as horror. After blockbuster special effects extravaganzas such as *Deep Impact* (1998), *Armageddon* (1998), and *The Day After Tomorrow* (2004), zombies poured onto our screens in hordes. Films such as *28 Days Later* (2002) and a remake of *Dawn of the Dead* (2004) were soon followed by zom-coms like *Shaun of the Dead* (2004), *Zombieland* (2009), and the zom-rom-com film *Warm Bodies* (2013). All of this was in addition to AMC's *The Walking Dead*, which began its long run in 2010.

There are many common characteristics of zombie films and TV shows, tropes so commonplace they've become clichéd. The idea that a zombie can only be killed by a blow to the head is hilariously lampooned in *Zombieland*'s repeated entreaty to "double tap" rather than assume a zombie was killed by the first shot. (The 2019 sequel, in fact, has "double tap" as its subtitle.) There's a format and a sameness to these movies, such that it's easy to wonder why audiences still hunger for them.

I'd suggest that the most important feature they have in common, what really connects with audiences, is the world they ask us to imagine and how this world intersects with our own. One reason zombies have become so popular is their ability to multiply and overrun. Once a zombie pandemic starts, it gets quickly out of control, and before long, there's not much of a society left. A few survivors are left to fend for themselves as best they can and develop new systems that will keep them alive after everything has collapsed.

It's probably not an accident that this formula surged in popularity in the early 2000s in the wake of the terrorist attacks of 9/11 and our attempts to figure out what the new "war on terror" meant for the world. *The Walking Dead* is based on a comic that debuted in 2003. Moreover, the television series debuted on Halloween 2010, just as America was digging itself out of the hole of the 2008 financial crisis. That period saw unemployment numbers that America hadn't witnessed in more than a quarter century; the real estate bubble had burst, leaving thousands of people defaulting on their mortgages. Countless families' savings dwindled, and young adults watched their prospects for meaningful employment disappear before their eyes. For many people, the American dream seemed more distant than it ever had.

The Walking Dead stepped into this uncertain cultural space. It wasn't exactly escapist entertainment—it was far too bleak for that. But it was entertainment that spoke to the anxiety and unrest so many people were feeling. Everything these characters had relied on for comfort and security was gone; every part of society they had taken for granted was no more. This forced them to ask the fundamental questions their viewers were also facing: When so much of life as we know it has vanished, what remains to hold on to? When nothing seems solid, what will get us through the day? What remains for us to hope for? I believe it's that fundamental question of hope that kept millions of viewers coming back to *The Walking Dead*. It's a question that seems so poignantly relevant after a financial collapse and as we try to put together the pieces of our world today. What is our hope?

Sometimes, when things are going well, we forget about hope entirely. We're focused on enjoying the moment, being proud of our accomplishments, and savoring material comforts. When life is easy, we forget how much *work* hope is. In those times, sometimes hope hangs around on its own, sitting next to us and patiently waiting. But as Emily Dickinson wrote, "Hope is the thing with feathers"—it can fly away if we're not careful. Hope is hardest to come by when we're walking through the valley of the shadow of death. We have to work for it.

When we immerse ourselves in a world like *The Walking Dead*, where hope is so elusive, we remember what it means to work for hope. We see the characters themselves toiling for it, and we see the consequences for the characters who give up or forget. In connecting with that part of ourselves, we can be inspired to find hope in our own lives, in places we might otherwise not have thought to look.

At times, holding on to hope takes both determination and creativity. A single-minded pursuit of hope can be all that gets us through the day, when we focus on one dream with an intensity that pushes other distractions aside. But sometimes, determination by itself isn't enough. In times of crisis, when the paths we've been pursuing have suddenly been closed off, we need to activate our creativity and find new sources of hope.

Sheriff Rick Grimes begins the first season of *The Walking Dead* with a blunt determination, thinking of nothing but reuniting with his family. When he succeeds, against all reasonable odds, he finds himself becoming a part of an ad hoc community of survivors who have learned how to adapt to their new environment. Their hope is rooted in the possibility of a safe, sustainable community that will provide for their basic needs as well as protect them from the ever-present "walkers." This hope eventually collapses as they realize their community doesn't have the resources it needs to protect itself. While there's of course some despair over this loss, the people exercise their resilience and creativity to find a new hope to support them. They show a remarkable ability to creatively adapt as circumstances change.

In the midst of crisis, this model of resilience and creativity in the service of hope is what we need to be reaching toward. In a strange way, watching the horrifying realities of life in the zombie apocalypse can be comforting. As we witness the faithful remnant trying to rebuild their lives out of the wreckage of a shattered society, we can think, "At least we're not alone." And as we watch these survivors struggle again and again to find new hope, we're able to reflect on the hope we can reach for in our own lives. In spite of its bleakness, *The Walking Dead* offers us a vision of grace.

In many ways, Psalm 23 and *The Walking Dead* are worlds apart. In contrast to the overwhelming dystopia of *The Walking Dead*, Psalm 23 presents a dream of comfort and rest, a hope of being safe and cared for. But it also recognizes that this journey often involves the valley of the shadow; no matter how strong our faith may be, we still make that shadow journey. The fuel that keeps us moving is hope. When the shadows around us are deepest, when hope seems furthest away, that's when we need it most.

To me, Psalm 23's vision of goodness and mercy hunting us down sounds like grace. Hope feels at times like hard work, but in an unexplained way, it's also pursuing us. Sometimes, if we stay open to its possibilities and keep walking forward, hope catches us from behind.

3

FAITH AGAINST THE DARKNESS

The Exorcist (William Friedkin, 1973)
The Last Exorcism (Daniel Stamm, 2010)
Girl on the Third Floor (Travis Stevens, 2019)

The last chapter talked about hope, the longing for something that is not yet present. This chapter turns to faith, which might be defined as the insistence that something beautiful does, in fact, exist right here and now, even in the absence of tangible evidence.

What does it mean to have faith? What can faith do for us, and why does it still matter in twenty-first-century America, a culture that is quickly becoming "postreligious" as people leave the pews at ever-increasing rates? In this chapter, we'll see that postchurch doesn't have to mean postfaith and that horror movies are one surprising place where personal faith stubbornly endures, even if religious institutions themselves don't offer much help against the forces of evil.

BAD CLERGY

Religion is often a source of ridicule in horror films. The village priest or pastor is usually ineffectual, a symbol of the patriarchal authorities who cannot understand that something outside their control might be threatening their neighbors. In *Hellraiser III: Hell on Earth* (1992), Joey is on the run from Pinhead and his gang of torture-loving cenobites. She ducks into a downtown church seeking sanctuary, but the presiding priest is incredulous, refusing to believe her story or that she is in any danger. At least, until Pinhead bursts through the doors. The overwhelmed priest is quickly dispatched; when he tries to hold up a crucifix to halt Pinhead's reign of terror, the cenobite laughs. Here, the small faith and limited worldview of this priest are no match for the great evil that strides through the church doors.[1]

In many more horror films, the church itself is the source of evil. There's the lycanthropic priest in 1985's *Silver Bullet* (adapted from a Stephen King novella) or the excommunicated priest who leads a cabal of Satanists in the hammy Christopher Lee vehicle *To the Devil a Daughter* (1976). And there's the supremely creepy nun who first makes her appearance in *The Conjuring 2* (2016) and then takes center stage in a haunted abbey in *The Nun* (2018). The hypocrisy and single-mindedness that have too often marked the church make it an easy target for horror films.

Also fitting loosely into this category of "bad clergy" is the protagonist of the "found-footage" horror film *The Last Exorcism* (2010), con man pastor and exorcist Cotton Marcus. Reverend Marcus has made his career by staging fake exorcisms. He believes that all the instances of demonic possession he has been called to remedy are a sham, though he acknowledges that many of the victims truly believe they are possessed. He conducts elaborate scam exorcisms to make victims and their families feel better, hoping to help the "possessed" individuals move beyond the mental illness that is causing them to act out. He's also enriching himself in the process, a snake oil salesman through and through. "Every preacher has to have a hook," he explains, "something that's going to bring the people in and get them saved." In a moment of honesty, he confides, "And frankly, get them in their wallets. The church doesn't run on love."

However, Cotton is such a con man that money isn't even his primary motivation. He loves the ego trip it gives him to fool people. He gleefully tells a documentary film crew that once he's gotten the people in the pews excited enough, they'll believe anything he tells them. He then proceeds to demonstrate this by enthusiastically yelling out his mom's banana bread recipe in the middle of a fiery sermon. Without breaking stride or changing his tone or cadence, the pastor draws out calls of "Amen!" and "Hallelujah!" from the congregation as he shouts about overripe bananas and the correct oven temperature. He smiles smugly at the camera, unable to suppress the pride he feels at his own showmanship. Cotton's very name harkens back to the church's well-known ability to influence people in less-than-desirable ways; it's a clear reference to Cotton Mather, the renowned preacher of Puritan New England whose writings played a large part in whipping up the frenzy that led to the Salem witch trials in 1692. Of course, by the end of the film, Cotton Marcus realizes that he is in over his head. He finds himself face to face with a real, honest-to-God case of demonic possession, which his lack of faith has left him ill-equipped to handle. This charlatan may have been able to fool the rubes, but he is no match for true evil.

Reverend Marcus is an extreme example of the horror film trope of jaded, ineffective clergy. But that's not the only story connected with clergy in the world of horror. Just as there's a long tradition of rotten clergy who have allowed the church to become corrupted, there are also clergy whose faith grants them particular strengths against the forces of darkness.

THE POWER OF BELIEF

The Gospel of Matthew recounts several stories about demonic possession, including one when a possessed man was brought to Jesus for healing. The poor man is described as having seizures so severe that "he often falls into the fire and into the water" (Matthew 17:15). Jesus's disciples don't have any luck, but Jesus (after chastising the "faithless and perverse generation" and wondering how long he'll have to put up with them), commands the demon to leave. The demon obeys immediately, and the man is cured. When the disciples ask why their efforts didn't succeed, Jesus tells them they failed "because of your little faith" (17:20). Jesus continues, "If you have faith the size of a mustard seed, you will say to this mountain, 'Move from here to there,' and it will move; nothing will be impossible for you."

The Gospels recount several other times when Jesus uses the example of a mustard seed, one of the smallest of all seeds but one that grows into a large, bush-like tree. Mysteriously, in Mark 4:31, Jesus compares the kingdom of God to a mustard seed, something so tiny as to be easily overlooked and dismissed but that grows into a tree large enough to shelter birds when it has been planted. In the Gospels, as in horror, deeply held faith is a powerful force.

From this we know that faith is important, and from the perspective of a religious worldview a person who has even a tiny amount of true, sincere faith can do amazing things. That makes sense at first, until we stop to think about what "faith" actually means, and what it means to "have" faith. Exactly what faith is can be hard to describe.

Sometimes, we make the mistake of thinking that faith is about agreeing to the correct set of assumptions about God or the way the world works. In this worldview, if someone agrees that Jesus is the Son of God, they have faith. Or if they believe that only people who hold certain religious views will get to heaven, they have faith. But I would suggest that doctrinal conformity is not the only way to understand what faith is, and is probably not the most helpful.

New Testament scholar Marcus Borg built his career on encouraging people to move from a childish, simplistic view of God to a more fully formed adult understanding. For Borg, part of the reason that so many people leave the church in their high school years and never come back is that the church does such a poor job of helping them move from a Sunday school faith into a mature set of beliefs where God and Santa Claus are easily distinguishable from one another and there's no old man in white robes sitting on a throne in the clouds.[2] For Borg, real faith is about trust. It means letting this trust guide the choices we make and our basic outlook on everything around us. As Borg puts it, faith is making the decision to believe that the universe is inherently good—and then living as if that is true.

That's a powerful statement with a lot to unpack. Borg doesn't claim that belief always lines up with reality. In his formulation, it might be the case that the universe isn't, in fact, inherently good, which is a possibility that many horror movies explore. The key is to decide to *live as if it were*. In this way, faith is not a series of agreements, but an attitude toward life and a trust in the basic goodness of the world. Thus, faith can deeply and profoundly change who we are, affecting every decision we make about our relationships, our vocations, what to do with our money, and how we find meaning in our lives. Faith really does matter, in ways much more profound than what we say on Sunday morning.

When we view faith in this manner—as a way of thinking about life rather than as a set of agreements about theological principles—it's easier to see the role that faith plays in horror.

One example comes in the figure of Father Damien Karras, the title character of *The Exorcist* (1973). When we first meet him, he's struggling. He's got a background in psychiatry, so he has one foot in the world of science and one in the world of religion. But he seems to have had problems at his last parish, so he's been reassigned to work with troubled priests. We get the sense that Father Karras's difficulties at his last parish might be related to his own crisis of faith; at the beginning of the film, he isn't sure what he believes in or if he believes in a higher power at all anymore. Father Karras is struggling with a loss of faith.

When he gets drawn into assisting with the exorcism of Regan, a young girl who has been displaying alarming demonic symptoms, Father Karras isn't sure that he's the right man. Mostly, he doesn't know if his faith is strong enough. The demon Pazuzu recognizes this in Father Karras, mocking him for the instance when he chose not to help a homeless man as well as pushing on Father Karras's lack of certainty regarding his recently deceased mother's final destination. (If you've seen the movie, you'll know that's a very nice way of putting it.) Father Karras finally achieves victory over the demon when he realizes that faith is not about what he believes may or may not be true, but how he acts. He demands that the demon leave Regan alone and enter him instead; the demon obliges, either out of playfulness or an inability to decline. Once the demon has entered him, Father Karras throws himself out the window, killing himself, but also banishing the demon.

Through this act of self-sacrifice, Father Karras reconnects with a central tenet of his Christian faith. In laying down his life to save the girl and expel the monster, he demonstrates the "no greater love" that Christ spoke about (John 15:13). In that single moment, Father Karras's crisis of faith has been resolved by the choice to live out his own teachings. He has decided to act as if the universe is inherently good, as if acts of self-sacrifice will be rewarded. That's a faith that Pazuzu can't withstand.

BELIEVING IN THE EVIL

In horror, belief cuts both ways. Belief can give people the power to fight the forces of evil, but it can also give that very evil more power. In fact, a number of horror films present an evil that only exists because people believe in it.

One such story is Andy Muschietti's overwrought two-part adaptation of Stephen King's *It* (2017, 2019). In the universe of *It*, a clown named Pennywise has haunted the town of Derry for generations and returns every few decades to find more young people to feast on. But the kids of the self-proclaimed Losers' Club have discovered Pennywise's weakness: he only has power so long as people are afraid of him. Both films conclude with the gang deciding to take Pennywise's power away, encircling him and taunting him as weak and powerless. (This is one of many aspects of the film that doesn't seem to be self-critical enough; I found it highly disturbing to see these bullied children rise up to mimic bullying behavior, even if it was against a malevolent clown-demon.) Belief is what gives Pennywise power; when the Losers' Club takes this belief away, he has nothing.

This motif shows up in the later Freddy Krueger movies as well, particularly in *Wes Craven's New Nightmare* (1994) and *Freddy vs. Jason* (2003). A few years after the *Nightmare on Elm Street* cash cow had run dry, creator Wes Craven tried to revive the sagging franchise with an ahead-of-its-time meta-horror film. He did this kind of self-reflexive horror film much more successfully a couple of years later with *Scream* (1996), but *New Nightmare* still has some interesting elements. It's a story that's built entirely on the idea that belief is powerful.

In Wes Craven's *New Nightmare*, Freddy is only a fictional character. Heather Langenkamp, star of the first *Nightmare* movie and with a major role in the third, plays herself as an actress working on a new Freddy movie. Wes Craven also portrays himself as a screenwriter who has written the movie she is filming. As Heather starts to have nightmares of Freddy, Wes confesses that the *Nightmare* movies have trapped an ancient evil, and he's worried that the only way to keep it contained is to continue making movies about it. This evil is trapped because people believe that Freddy is only a character in a movie. As long as they persist in this belief, that's all he'll be. But once the films stop being made, the evil can escape into the real world. When they make the new movie, people will return to believing that Freddy isn't real, and he won't have any power. It's a brilliant way to comment on how our belief has the power to make things real.

While *New Nightmare* explores the power of belief to contain evil, *Freddy vs. Jason* (2003) suggests that belief is what evil feeds on. The film is a fan's dream in which the villains of the *Nightmare on Elm Street* and *Friday the 13th* franchises combine forces to increase their death toll but end up in a cage match–style brawl at the end. It hasn't held up well; in an attempt to give a new edge to Freddy's witticisms, several of his taunts invoke race or sexual assault, and one of his victims mocks the killer with a homophobic slur. It was not one of the high points of early 2000s horror cinema, and it looks even more regrettable with the passage of time. Even so, some of the plot's features are interesting in light of this chapter's discussion.

As the film begins, Jason is in hell—if you really need to know how that happened, you can watch the 1993 pic *Jason Goes to Hell: The Final Friday*, though I wouldn't recommend it—and Freddy is powerless because no one believes in him anymore. In a rather half-baked plan, Freddy finds a way to resurrect Jason and set him loose in Freddy's hometown; the idea is that once people start dying, they'll remember Freddy's own glory days of murder and mayhem, and Freddy can get back to his old tricks again. The plan works, at least for the first part of the film. Once the town is afraid of Freddy again, he has the power to return to haunt them once more. But he only has that power so long as they believe in him. Eventually, however, Jason starts killing enough people that they're more afraid of him than of Freddy, and the slasher-on-slasher battle begins. This is the flip side of the faithful warriors motif explored previously: just as belief can give power to the forces of good, it can also empower evil. Belief is power in and of itself.

Helpful People, Unhelpful Church

Even though individual faithful warriors, like Father Karras in *The Exorcist*, often play heroic roles in horror, it's rare that the institutional church comes out well. Since the release of *The Exorcist*, as Americans' trust in religious institutions has continued to decline, this trend has only accelerated. While the universe of *The Conjuring*, mentioned at the start of this chapter, takes questions of good and evil very seriously, the people who wield faith in defense of others are frequently on the margins of the church and have to work against its unwieldy bureaucracy. In the first *Conjuring* (2013), Ed and Lorraine Warren are laypeople who have assisted with exorcisms before. They're pressed into service by the imminent danger the Perron family finds themselves in. Ed decides to perform the exorcism ritual on his own, without assistance or ecclesiastical authorization. Only after the exorcism has been accomplished and the Perron family is saved does Ed receive a call from the Vatican informing him that the exorcism has been approved.

Similarly, in *The Curse of La Llorona* (2019), another entry into the loosely connected "Conjuring Universe," the Tate-Garcia family is under siege from the ghost of a "Weeping Woman" and seek help from a priest named Father Perez. Father Perez is unable to help them, citing the regulations of the church, but directs them to Rafael Olvera, a former priest who has no such restrictions. Because Rafael is unbound by the church's hierarchy, he is able to perform the rituals necessary to defend the family. If there is one dominant position of the horror genre as it relates to religion, it might be this: there is a deep, abiding truth to the reality of the spiritual world, and spirituality can be used as a tool to fight against the forces of evil. But more often than not, the institution of the church itself stands in the way.

This is seldom made more explicit than in *Stigmata* (1999). The film follows a young woman, Frankie, who becomes afflicted with inexplicable wounds on her wrists and then feels herself being whipped violently by an unseen force. You'll probably notice that this is yet another film where a woman is victimized and a male priest attempts to come to her rescue. This kind of gender essentialism is a persistent problem in horror films. As we'll see later in the book, there are some counterexamples that turn this stereotype on its head, but much of the history of horror is stuck in the tropes of a victimized woman who must be saved (or not) by a patriarchal man. Film scholar Carol Clover noted in her book *Men, Women, and Chain Saws* how often horror movies center on a man's crisis of faith being played out over the body of a woman; the woman is almost superfluous to the heroic journey that the male undertakes.[3]

Stigmata is a characteristic example of this problem. The victimized Frankie receives aid from Father Andrew Kiernan, who has experience investigating miracles. (Father Kiernan is played by Gabriel Byrne, who also portrayed the devil in *End of Days* the same year. I can't think of a better way to hedge your bets.) Father Kiernan is an investigator of unexplained phenomena for the church, another example of a religious man equally at home in the realm of science. He is also suffering a faith crisis, a plot device that comes straight out of *The Exorcist*'s playbook. He becomes convinced that Frankie is experiencing the stigmata—wounds delivered by God to imitate the suffering of Christ. Usually, this phenomenon is only given to the deeply faithful; Father Kiernan is baffled that Frankie is suffering from it, since she is an avowed atheist. Lucky Frankie.

In this film, the horror comes directly from God, not from a force of evil struggling against the divine will. God is inflicting pain on the body of this innocent woman in order to present a message: when Father Kiernan comes to check on her, he finds her scrawling on her apartment walls, in blood, what seems to be a very ancient Gospel. It turns out to be something like the Gospel of Thomas, a noncanonical text that was rediscovered in 1945 outside of Egypt, as part of the Nag Hammadi library of religious texts from around the fourth century CE. Many of the Nag Hammadi texts were not included in the Bible. Thomas presents a different vision of Jesus and the church than the Gospels that have been preserved in the Bible, focusing primarily on the individual's direct relationship with God. It has sometimes been referred to as a gnostic document because of the way it promises each believer direct access to secret knowledge. The early church decided it didn't need this Gospel; it wasn't included with the group of books that the church determined would make up the Bible, and most copies of it were destroyed.

In *Stigmata*, however, the Catholic Church's suppression of this document is ongoing, intentional, and conspiratorial. In the film's climax, Father Kiernan realizes that Frankie has been possessed by the spirit of a priest who was excommunicated for continuing to work on a translation of this text against the Roman Catholic Church's orders. God is using Frankie to make sure the work he gave this priest can come to fruition. (Here we have the female's suffering sidelined by not one but two male priests!) As opposed to being possessed by an evil demon, Frankie has been possessed by a priest God has empowered to publicize the truth in spite of the church's restrictions. The truth that Frankie has been compelled to deliver is a simple one: "the kingdom of God is inside you and all around you, not in mansions of wood and stone." This seems to combine two quotations from the Gospel of Thomas.[4]

Stigmata presents a world in which this truth is so dangerous that the institution of the Catholic Church would go to great lengths to suppress it. In reality, when the Gospel of Thomas was rediscovered in 1945, the Catholic Church (along with most other denominations) found it to offer compelling insights into the nonorthodox sects of Christianity's early years, when everyone was still figuring out exactly what the religion's doctrine would look like. But that kind of nuanced response doesn't make for very good entertainment. It's much more exciting to have an evil, manipulative religious organization pulling strings from the shadows in a malevolent attempt to consolidate its own power.

That is an extreme example, and it puts *Stigmata* more readily into the company of books like *The Celestine Prophecy* or *The Da Vinci Code*. Even though the conspiracies woven into these stories are hard to believe, churches often behave in ways that lend them some credence. It's easy to think of headlines from the past decades involving a prominent televangelist who redirected believers' offerings to fund his own luxurious lifestyle or conservative preachers who railed against homosexuality and promiscuity only to get caught up in their own sex scandals. And perhaps more chillingly, there is the story of the Romanian convent that became convinced one of its sisters was possessed by a demon and tried to perform an emergency exorcism. In reality, the young woman was suffering from schizophrenia, but the brutal methods of the local church led to her death. (This was hauntingly dramatized in the 2012 film *Beyond the Hills*.) When churches behave like this in real life, it's easy to believe the worst in a movie.

But more frequently in horror, religious organizations are bureaucratic, and far too slow to respond to the evil that is happening right before the characters' eyes. In this way, religion aligns itself with the bumbling sheriff who doesn't believe the kids when a blob has landed from outer space or that there's a killer on the loose at Camp Crystal Lake (*Friday the 13th*). Or with the parents who think their terrified kids are just telling stories, oblivious to the monster that's outside. Authority figures usually don't fare well in horror movies, and the church is no exception. You might say that horror movies, along with the rest of American culture, have become increasingly "spiritual but not religious."

Sometimes, however, the church gets its act together and can become a powerful force in the fight against evil. A hilarious example comes from *Night of the Demons 2* (1994), in which a religious school finds itself under assault by a host of demons.

The nuns rally, filling super-soakers with holy water. The demons learn firsthand what thousands of people learned as kids in Catholic school: you don't mess with the sisterhood.

A more serious reflection on the church's role in an increasingly postreligious world can be found in *Girl on the Third Floor* (2019). Much of the film involves a setup shared with any number of haunted house narratives; the main distinction is that rather than a new family moving into a haunted house, Don (played by former pro wrestler Phil Brooks) has moved in by himself with plans to renovate the home before his wife joins him. Don has problems with infidelity, drinking, robbery, and lying, and he's hoping that turning this fixer-upper into a dream home for his wife will paper over his past mistakes. But the house has been vacant for years because of its sordid past: it used to be a brothel, and one of the prostitutes went missing. (One guess as to where she is eventually found.)

What's most interesting is the character of Pastor Ellie, whose church is located across the street. The first time we see Ellie, she is standing at Don's door with a bottle of bourbon to share. At first, all she offers him is a friendly conversation and an invitation: "My door is always open—if you care to learn more." Later in the film, she comes back after Don has been struggling with the forces inside the house. Sitting on the porch with him again, she asks, "Do you wanna talk about it?" Don rebuffs her at first, before acknowledging that he's been having a rough time. "I bet," Ellie says. "This house is a bitch." Don can only tell her that he's trying to rebuild his marriage and become a better person, in a manner that reveals he doesn't have a lot of confidence in his abilities. "Blessed is the man who remains steadfast," she tells him, reverting into pastor mode. Not long after this conversation, Don will find himself becoming another of the house's ghosts.

Ellie has been the neighborhood pastor for thirty-five years, and we find out that she's watched several families try to build a life in the house. But, as Ellie has learned, the house has a way of revealing people's true nature. After Don goes missing, his wife, Liz, comes looking for him. Pastor Ellie stops by for a conversation with her as well, also on the front porch. Here, we get the sense that Ellie isn't willing to step inside. "This house has a history of . . . bringing out the worst in people," she says. "I just want to make sure you two are prepared for that." Liz listens politely but isn't too interested in what the pastor has to say. She's mostly concerned with finding her husband.

After the true evil of the house, as well as her husband's fate, has been revealed to Liz, she has one last conversation with the reverend on the porch. "You knew!" she accuses Ellie, demanding to know why she didn't tell them. Ellie admits knowing that evil resided in the house and that she understood the choices Don and Liz were facing. But Ellie also understands that these were choices that Don and Liz had to make themselves and that the house's ghostly prostitutes have their own power. "I can't keep anyone out of this house," she tells Liz, "any more than those girls can keep anyone out of mine." Like many haunted houses, the house in this film feeds on the unhappiness and anger of its current occupants; Don didn't have the strength of character to avoid being swallowed by it. In *Girl on the Third Floor*, the church is across the street from the evil house, a short walk away. The church is open to anyone. It understands the nature of evil and what people have to do to avoid horrible fates. But the church is also aware of the limitations of its power; its true influence is indirect. In this worldview, the church doesn't act with overwhelming force, crushing evil under its heel. Instead, it waits patiently, hoping people will make the right choices. It stands as a possibility that's always available. It's a much more humble, realistic understanding of what the church is and is not able to accomplish in this world.

This takes us back to the definition of faith we wrestled with at the beginning of the chapter. Faith isn't about a willingness to agree to certain ideas; it's an overall openness toward life, and a commitment to living out that attitude in the world. Faith means deciding that something outside of ourselves is important and worthy of our commitment. It could be God, it could be our fellow humans, it could be the natural world. But when we have faith, we can no longer view ourselves as the most important thing in the world. If faith means anything, it means the end of selfishness.

In the end, faith is a choice. What we choose to believe in gives us power, for good or for ill. When we choose to believe in something good, whether that's a loving god or the kindness of humanity, it gives us power to do great things. It's all about the choices we make.

4

FEARFULLY AND WONDERFULLY

PRECHAPTER VIEWING RECOMMENDATIONS

Pure (Hannah Macpherson, 2019)
Black Christmas (Sophia Takal, 2019)

O ur bodies are amazing pieces of machinery. The sheer number of parts that work with one another, the complex tasks they can accomplish, the sensations they produce, and how they all work together in a functioning whole are simply astonishing to think about. As Psalm 139 says, we are "fearfully and wonderfully made."

But as we move through life, at some time or another, we'll have experiences that cause us to reflect more deeply on how vulnerable these bodies are. Depending on your personal experience and life history, this may be something you've known intimately for a long time. But if you've been reasonably healthy throughout your life, you may be tempted to view your body as a Timex, a piece of machinery that will keep on ticking no matter what life throws at it. Sooner or later, though, something will happen to shake you out of that daydream.

This vulnerability asserts itself in other ways, too. Our bodies' needs for things like food and sex generate a different kind of vulnerability. We see this in the way so many religious traditions try to regulate how bodies behave, draw boundaries about which types of bodies belong, or valorize bodies they view as perfect or pure. Horror frequently addresses these anxieties more directly, often by depicting the vulnerability of the body in graphic images. These vastly different expressions still give voice to a shared concern: our bodies are who we are, and they are terrifyingly fragile. Horror and religion both have a multitude of resources for helping us think through these problematic questions—some helpful and life-giving, some less so. In the "less helpful" category, both horror and religion are also preoccupied with policing the boundaries of acceptable sexuality.

HORROR AND THE BODY

As mentioned in chapter 1, Hollywood film production from the mid-1930s to the late 1960s was governed by a set of rules known as the Hays Code.[1] In terms of how it affected depictions of the body, sections provided specific bans on depictions of content that was deemed to be sexually aberrant (such as homosexuality, adultery, or interracial marriage, then known as miscegenation). Writers and directors worked to ensure that respect for the law was always upheld. If characters did something the code viewed as bad, they had to be punished for it by the end of the film. Under the strict rules of the Hays Code, horror had to be implied, explicit gore was minimal, and the main characters' bodies stayed largely intact. As the Hays Code broke down, so did horror's respect for the integrity of the body.

Another interesting development in the film industry led to the sea changes movies would experience in the 1960s. Until the 1940s, the movie studios also owned theater chains and had complete control over what was distributed. But in 1948, the Supreme Court outlawed these "vertical monopolies" in *United States v. Paramount Pictures, Inc.*, forcing theater chains to become independent of the studios.[2] This opened the door for independent, non-studio-produced films, which slowly gained momentum throughout the 1960s. The independent film movement and the collapse of the Hays Code crashed into each other in the 1960s, leading to film content that hadn't been seen in America before.

Herschell Gordon Lewis's notorious (and frankly lousy) 1963 film *Blood Feast* was the first to fully imagine the potential of a horror cinema unconstrained by production codes, social norms, or general standards of decency. The explicit depictions of decapitations, amputations, tongue-severings, and other nastiness hadn't been shown on-screen before, and the film's marketing campaign tapped into this by offering cinemagoers vomit bags. Playing mainly at drive-ins, the film sold about $4 million worth of tickets, a healthy profit over its $24,500 production cost. Lewis made several other films in this same vein: low-budget, trashy affairs with little attention paid to acting, cinematography, or plot. These films are primarily concerned with a fascination about what can happen to bodies.

The next major milestone in the vulnerability of the body in horror occurred a few years later, when George Romero made gore an integral part of a film that had many other elements to recommend it. *Night of the Living Dead* (1968), discussed in the introduction and again in chapter 2, was shocking for its carnage, particularly the scene where the living dead are seen chomping down on the intestines and organs of a recent victim. But this butchery was in the service of a compelling and tense story, driven by a tightly crafted script and some very good performances, particularly from lead actor Duane Jones. In *Night*, the gore feels like a natural outgrowth of the film's plot and theme, a way for Romero to increase the tension dramatically at key moments rather than the entire point of the film. And even more than increasing tension, it served as a way for Romero to explore the thematic elements that *Night* was centered around.

In many ways, *Night* is a reflection on how vulnerable we all are—as a species, as family units, and as individuals. The film takes place during the course of a single night, during which we see society's disintegration through newscasts and radio clips; the film's conclusion then offers the result of this disintegration, as a band of vigilantes whoops it up while shooting their way through the zombie-filled landscape. The family unit fares no better, as depicted in the Cooper family. Patriarch Harry tries to take control of the situation but doesn't offer much except arguing that the cellar is a safer place than the house's main floor. His wife, Helen, is dismissive of his macho bluster, seemingly resigned to the reality that her husband can offer her no protection. Harry also can't shield the family's young daughter, who is bitten by one of the ghouls. Eventually, she turns into a ghoul herself, killing her mother with a gardening trowel. The family, unable to hold itself together, is destroyed from within by its own members. The scene is the same elsewhere; a young couple showcased in the film are at least kinder to each other, but their relationship proves unable to save them from becoming food.

The film brings into sharp focus the vulnerability of the individual characters and the fragile nature of their bodies. The society they have trusted has fallen apart and cannot keep them safe. The families and romantic relationships they are a part of cannot keep them safe. All that's between them and the horde of living dead outside are the thin walls of a farmhouse and the boards nailed over its windows. As we see the living dead feasting on the inward parts of the young couple, or Helen being slaughtered by her own daughter, we're vividly aware of what it means to be a fragile human, to have bodies that can break open and cease to hold us together.

The ease with which our own bodies can be destroyed is one source of anxiety; being responsible for other people's physical destruction is another. While the horror genre has featured graphic depictions of bodily harm and torture since Lewis's films of the 1960s, the first time films of this nature gained widespread, mainstream popularity in the United States was in the mid-2000s, with so-called torture porn films. Films like *Saw* (2004) and *Hostel* (2005) spent a good part of their running time depicting pain being inflicted on bound or otherwise helpless individuals, forcing audiences to squirm in their seats for minutes at a time while terrible things happened to a captive person on-screen. In many of these films, the tension arose less from whether the characters could escape death than from how much suffering they (and, by extension, the audience) would be forced to endure.

It makes perfect sense that these films would break into the mainstream right as our national conversation was engulfed with the horrors of Abu Ghraib and "enhanced interrogation" techniques, which became public knowledge in 2004. Americans grappled with what this appalling treatment of detainees meant for our nation. Was this just the ugly side of keeping us safe, a necessary evil that had always been present but had previously simmered under the surface? Or was something new and different happening, making our nation morally culpable in ways we hadn't been before? (Or at least hadn't realized we were before.) As unpleasant as these films are, many of them explore questions of culpability and agency in ways that reflect on our national sense of responsibility for the bodily horrors that we learned were being committed in our names.

This is most clear in *Hostel*. This deeply unpleasant film follows a pair of American college students on an overseas trip, looking for booze and sex. They're not very likeable, exhibiting many of the behaviors that have come to define toxic masculinity and stereotypes of the Ugly American. When they learn of a war-torn village in eastern Europe where, supposedly, there aren't enough men to satisfy the carnal desires of the female population, they head there immediately. They check into the local hostel on arrival, finding a bacchanalian paradise of available young women. However, the two backpackers quickly learn that they've fallen into a trap; the women of the hostel are working on commission for an underground club that gives billionaires the opportunity to torture a victim for a large fee. The price depends on the nationality of the victim, and torturing an American is the most expensive option. While we may be horrified by the punishment meted out, there's an underlying sense that these entitled Americans are receiving their payback from the rest of the world.

In this way, the violence of *Hostel* connects with early twenty-first-century anxieties over how easily immense harm can be inflicted to bodies and what it means that this kind of harm has been done on our behalf. I hesitate to recommend this film to anyone and definitely not to the squeamish. Even so, its popularity in the mid-2000s has profound implications for America's state of mind in the wake of 9/11 and Abu Ghraib.

BIBLICAL BODIES

Christianity obviously features a great deal of talk about the soul. Partially in response to the philosophy of Hellenistic Greece, which saw the body as a temporary house for the soul, Christianity has placed importance on the soul as the part of us that endures, where the true self is held. Although such a sharp division between the soul and the body is alien to the thinking of the Hebrew Bible, most scholars think this idea entered Christianity most directly through the writings of Paul. In this view, the body is only a shell, protecting the soul until it escapes this world.

The problem is that the body is a very fragile suit of armor for the soul to reside in. It doesn't offer much protection. As a result, the soul can be damaged by the vulnerabilities of the body. There are two main ways that this dynamic plays out in Christian discourse, both with interesting relevance to horror films.

The first is in Christianity's embrace of the ways in which the body can be physically broken, such as in the martyr stories of the early Christian period and the Middle Ages. In these stories, the body being broken was a way for the soul to demonstrate its virtue. This strand of thinking continues into the twenty-first century, as demonstrated by the enormous success of Mel Gibson's brutally violent, and virulently anti-Semitic, *The Passion of the Christ* (2004). Even though the breaking of the body is sometimes viewed as a way to "witness" (the literal reading of the Greek word from which we get "martyr") to God, these stories tap into the fear we have of the destruction of our bodies. Through graphic depictions of bodily mutilation, burning, and other forms of torture, early martyr stories ask readers to gaze deeply into their worst imaginings. "And if the people undergoing these torments can stay faithful to God," these stories seem to admonish, "it should be easy for you!" In Christian accounts of believers being tortured for the sake of

God, fear of the broken body becomes a way to encourage faith among those who aren't suffering such calamities.

The second way that bodily vulnerability is expressed in many strands of contemporary Christianity occurs through concerns over sexuality. The fear is not so much that the body is vulnerable to damage as it is prey to temptation. Individuals who succumb to sexual desire and seduction can act in ways that damage the soul. Our bodies can lead us astray, either in thought or in deed, putting the soul in jeopardy.

I should pause here to mention that I think this is a less-than-healthy approach, and there are many Christian traditions that agree with me. Figuring out how to make peace with the vulnerabilities of the body—expressed both as the potential to have harm done to it and its needs and desires—should be one of the purposes of any religious tradition. But when concerns about the body are reduced to simplistic, moralistic questions of right and wrong desires, rather than viewing these decisions as existing in a complex ethical network involving ourselves, other people, and the world, we do a disservice to our lived experience. And when we try to force those anxieties on others, either through moral or legal pressure, we spread that damage around. So, as I hope will become clear in this discussion, I'm not advocating for this viewpoint. I'm merely describing it as one that exists, has a great hold over much of contemporary American Christianity, and can reveal some memorable insights about our anxieties as human beings.

There's certainly some biblical basis for this understanding of the body as dangerous to the sanctity of the soul. Perhaps most directly is the apostle Paul, writing in his first letter to the early church at Corinth, where he cautions them: "Shun fornication! Every sin that a person commits is outside the body; but the fornicator sins against the body itself. Or do you not know that your body is a temple of the Holy Spirit within you, which you have from God, and that you are not your own?" (1 Corinthians 6:18–20). This is part of a lengthy diatribe Paul unleashes on the members of the Corinthian church for what seems to have been rampant immorality. Although Paul touches on issues such as theft, idolatry, and drunkenness, illicit sex is his greatest concern.

In this letter, Paul makes clear that he views sins of sexuality as being on a different level than other sins. Other sins are "outside the body"—they arise from the ways we interact with the world, how we treat each other, or even what we allow ourselves to think. But in Paul's formulation, unauthorized sex is unique in that it involves the individual sinning against their own body and, in doing so, drawing themselves away from God. The body is a "temple" that protects the soul within.

This kind of thinking has led sexuality to be an obsession for Evangelical Christians. The early Reformers—theologians such as Martin Luther and John Calvin who broke with the Catholic Church and started the Protestant movement in the sixteenth century—believed that people were inherently sinful ("depraved," in the words of Calvin) and that only God's grace could provide salvation. But starting with the Holiness movements in the eighteenth century, many Christian groups found a renewed interest in the individual's ability to "sanctify" him- or herself through devotion and right action. Individual believers had the capacity to influence their own salvation by abstaining from liquor and other pleasures of the world, including premarital sex. Especially premarital sex.

In more modern times, Holiness-inspired "purity" movements within Evangelicalism took off in the 1970s and 1980s. These groups placed a huge emphasis on abstaining from sex until marriage—particularly for young women. As young men, pop stars the Jonas Brothers wore purity rings, indicating that they were promising to save themselves for marriage. Sometimes, Evangelical Christians hold events like Daddy-Daughter Purity Balls, in which daughters promise their fathers that they'll stay virgins until marriage, and their fathers pledge to protect their virginity. Linda Kay Klein, author of the memoir *Pure*, notes that such events aren't a huge part of mainstream evangelical culture; what is more common is the insidious and insistent message to young women that their bodies are not their own.[3] And that the decisions they make with their bodies—or, perhaps, allow their bodies to make for them—have a huge bearing on the eternal destination of their souls.

The 2019 film *Pure*, an entry into Hulu's Into the Dark series, explores the horror of this subculture and serves as a larger reflection on Evangelicals' anxiety over the purity of the body. It's set at a "Purity Camp," in which dads and daughters spend a few days together in the woods, culminating in a ball where they sign pledges with each other. Even before the demon Lilith shows up, the humiliation these young women endure at the hands of controlling men is painful to watch. A memorable scene occurs during one of the camp's morning worship sessions. Pastor Seth asks Shay if she likes gum, holding out a piece to her. "Right now," the pastor says, "it is as it should be. Brand new and fresh." But then he pops it into his mouth and chews demonstratively, pacing around the stage as he enjoys the gum's flavor. He then pulls the piece out and offers it to Shay. When she shakes her head no, he launches into his sermon. "Nobody wants that!" he tells the congregation. "Because it's been used." He drops the piece of gum on the floor as worthless trash to be discarded.

The message to young women is clear: You only have value to the extent that you are free from the stain of sexual contact with other people (or even yourself—masturbation is also verboten). Your body does not belong to you. It is on loan to you from your father, to be preserved until it is given over to your husband, and finally returned to God at the end of life. In all this, your obligation is to restrain your body from acting on the desires that would otherwise do harm to your soul. (You also have to protect the souls of young men, since they can't be expected to control their own sexual desires.) It's a vision of life that easily leads to overwhelming anxiety, terrible self-esteem, and a rejection of many things that make us human.

Unsurprisingly, it's a worldview that's reflected—and sometimes challenged—in horror movies as well.

SEX AND THE HORROR FILM

Horror films are also deeply concerned with questions of sexuality and sometimes demonstrate similar fears over how expressions of sexuality can be controlled. This crept into horror long before sex could be depicted on-screen. In Tod Browning's *Dracula* (1931), the count has his sights set on Mina, a young woman engaged to John Harker. Dracula is the force that threatens heterosexual marriage and tries to wrest Mina away. One of the underlying horrors of *Dracula* is the fear that this monster will be able to entice (white) women, causing them to stray from their domestic destiny and pursue the monstrous pleasures of a vampiric life. In the black-and-white films of the 1930s, this fear comes to the forefront repeatedly: Frankenstein's monster barges in on Dr. Frankenstein's wedding night to try to steal his bride away, and King Kong is the beast who tries to abduct an American beauty. In many of these films, the monster, frequently coded as a racialized Other, is the force that threatens white heterosexual marriage and in at least some instances (like *Dracula*) might be more appealing to the woman than her groom-to-be.

This anxiety became much more explicit with the slasher films of the 1980s, starting with John Carpenter's 1978 independent film *Halloween*. The film famously starts off with a shot from the point of view of an unknown character who watches as a young woman says goodbye to someone we presume to be her boyfriend. In the same shot, we continue to observe events through this unknown character's perspective: we are wandering through a house, picking up a knife, and then heading upstairs to murder this young woman, who is now only half-dressed. The shot ends with the revelation that the killer is a young boy who has just butchered his older sister. We have all the themes of the slasher film encapsulated in this short scene. As an audience, our point of view is, at least initially, aligned with the killer—we see through his eyes. The killer lashes out over expressions of sexuality, which encourages us as audience members to take a moralistic stance toward the behavior as well. Of course, the on-screen depictions of sexuality are also titillating, so we get to enjoy participating in this while also staying at a moral distance. And the audience's identification with the killer is never complete, so we don't have to feel too guilty about getting inside his mind. It's a disturbing set of associations. *Halloween* set the template that franchises like *Friday the 13th* would milk for major box-office dollars throughout the 1980s, as would dozens of low-budget imitators, taking advantage of the new VHS format to bypass theaters and get their movies straight into video stores.

It's always seemed strange to me that conservative family-values groups have protested these films, like the nationwide protests against *Silent Night, Deadly Night* (1984) that were briefly discussed in chapter 1. In reality, slasher films align well with a religiously conservative worldview: they view transgressions against the rules of patriarchal society as being punishable by death and regard the problems of contemporary American society as being the result of too many kids without strong parental figures. Women who don't comply with the rules of patriarchal society often face particularly harsh punishments. When you think of it that way, it seems like something Jerry Falwell should be able to endorse.

But it's also a formula that can be easily undercut and repurposed for different ends. A great example of this is the 2019 film *Black Christmas*. It's a loose remake of Bob Clark's classic 1974 film of the same name, about a group of sorority sisters being menaced by an obscene phone caller who turns deadly. This earlier film is the first time that the urban legend trope of "The calls are coming from inside the house!" arose in a horror movie. It inspired *Halloween*, though John Carpenter dialed down the character development and cranked up the fear of sexuality. Pretty much all that the 2019 remake has in common with its source material is the basic premise of sorority girls being stalked by a killer—this time via text rather than obscene calls. It's the rationale behind these killings that makes this update so interesting.

In every slasher film, the victims are chosen because they behave in ways that make the killer feel threatened or uncomfortable. Throughout the 1980s, this was frequently a fear of sex and feelings of arousal. Like Norman Bates in *Psycho* (1960), whose violent impulses kick into gear after he peeps on Marion Crane before her fateful shower, the slasher is frequently thrown into a rage by sex. Sometimes, films put this right on the surface—while it was already (barely concealed) subtext in the semicomic *The Slumber Party Massacre* (1982), as the killer's weapon of choice is an enormous, compensatory power drill, in *Slumber Party Massacre III* (1990), the killer is slaughtering nubile young women in reaction to his own experiences of impotence. In the straight-to-video slasher *Happy Hell Night* (1992), the killer murders a young woman taking a postcoital shower; before stabbing her, he tells her (and the audience): "No sex." It's a pattern that holds true for just about every slasher film of that era: sex is bad, and the young people who participate in it, especially the women, are going to get punished.

But in the 2019 version of *Black Christmas*, the relationship to sex is radically different. In this film, a sorority is being targeted by a masked killer; the revelation comes when we learn that these young women are not being targeted for *having* sex, but for pushing back against inappropriate and abusive sexual behavior on the part of one of the college's fraternities. The women are killed because they were advocating for gender balance in course reading lists or publicly calling out fraternity brothers who had sexually assaulted them. In the world of *Black Christmas*, advocating for equality is the true violation of sexual norms. There's no ambivalence about whose side we're supposed to be on in this film—evil is embodied by the fraternity brothers, the college that supports them, and the patriarchy they serve. It's easy to see *Black Christmas* as announcing a strand of horror for the #MeToo era.

This connects with the other major difference between *Black Christmas* and many of the slashers that came before: their attitude toward the "victims." In many slasher films, perhaps most notably those in the *Friday the 13th* cycle, the characters are portrayed as obnoxious, entitled, and generally without sympathetic qualities. For many audience members, part of the film's pleasure comes from watching these horrible people meet nasty ends. There's often one "Final Girl" who stands outside of these cliques. Jamie Lee Curtis's character in *Halloween* is the classic example: she doesn't participate in the sexual shenanigans and debaucheries that her friends are engaged in and therefore can stand as a heroine in the film's final scenes. But in *Black Christmas*, the characters are all imminently likeable—as an audience, we're clearly on their side. Rather than having a Final Girl who stands apart from her peers, the characters in *Black Christmas* come together at the end to fight back. Here, the horror the monster represents isn't premarital sex; it's sexual assault and other forms of patriarchal domination. When the characters fight back against the killer(s), they're opposing this entire system of injustice. It's a clear example of horror as a means of imagining another world—a topic we'll address more directly when we discuss questions of justice and the positive role that doubt can play.

Even with all this negativity around the body, it's possible to find examples of both horror and religion that offer a more positive way of relating to our bodies or at least push back on the negative patterns observed in evangelical purity culture and slasher films. In much of modern Christianity, sexuality is viewed as one of life's most important gifts—an important responsibility to be sure, but one that individuals are allowed to make their own decisions about, without the terrifying fear that a mistake will send them tumbling into an eternal abyss. Sexuality is a part of ourselves that we think about and respond to throughout our lives, in complex ways that often can't be dictated by a strict set of unbending rules.

In horror movies, there's almost always a monstrous figure (either an honest-to-goodness monster or a human with monstrous qualities), who represents something uncomfortable about our world. Robin Wood, recalling Sigmund Freud, refers to this as "the return of the repressed"—the monster is a part of our culture, a part of ourselves, that we wish would go away.[4] The monster comes back to remind us that it's still here. In movies like *Halloween* or *Friday the 13th*, the monster is the authoritarian impulse, the patriarchy that comes roaring back after years of civil rights protests and the loosening of social norms. (Slasher films became popular right as the Reagan Revolution was coming into its own.) But in *Pure* and the remake of *Black Christmas*, we saw models of horror movies where repressive or abusive sexuality was the monster-behind-the-monster. Instead of seeing the world through the killer's eyes, as in the "stalker cam" that *Halloween* made famous, the point of view stays with the films' heroines. And instead of characters who are portrayed as vain, shallow, and selfish—such that we even breathe a sigh of relief when they meet the sharp end of the slasher's blade—these films offer us heroines who are strong-willed, look out for each other, and are struggling honestly to find their place in the world. When Pastor Seth of *Pure* preaches that the proper response to female sexuality is repressive control, the film makes clear that this worldview is where the true monstrosity lies. Similarly, *Black Christmas* places the film's heroines against a group of misogynistic, abusive frat boys who are portrayed as the most recent in the long story of patriarchal oppression. There's no sympathy for these devils—a theme we'll explore in the next chapter, when we contemplate the nature of the monster.

5

"THEY'RE US . . ."

The Hills Have Eyes (Wes Craven, 1977—if you're
feeling brave!)
The Witch (Robert Eggers, 2015)

When we imagine monsters, we think of a horrifying beast, perhaps a giant, unnatural combination of animals with glistening teeth and a hungry mouth. It lurks in the darkness, waiting to pounce on us when we leave the comforts of our home. Or maybe it makes a quick incursion into the village to sneak through a window and snatch some human prey before running back to the shadows. The monster is, by definition, unhuman. Its body doesn't look anything like a person, its appetites and desires are far outside our understanding, and it lives in places where people don't go. The monster is what we are not.

But what if the monster isn't the Creature from the Black Lagoon or Godzilla but Norman Bates? What if, instead of being a horrifying beast, the monster looks like our next-door neighbor? Or what if, instead of a shambling zombie, the monster is an educated gourmand, like Hannibal Lecter in *The Silence of the Lambs* (1991), or a wealthy corporate executive, like Patrick Bateman in *American Psycho* (2000)? Monsters are not restricted to horror films; we see them on the nightly news. We've collectively witnessed how the monster can be a police officer kneeling on the neck of an unarmed citizen. Perhaps even more insidiously, the monster is the cultural and political system that has underwritten these oppressions for generations. While we try to pretend that the monster is outside, somewhere else, that's often a fantasy we tell ourselves to feel safe at night. If we're honest, we know that monsters live in our own communities and inside ourselves.

Horror and religion both give us a strong sense of the monstrous and encourage us to reflect critically on where it is located, whether without or within. When Paul laments that he is unable to do the good that he wishes to do, he is recognizing the monstrous within himself. "For I know that nothing good dwells within me," Paul says (Romans 7:18). It's why Norman Bates is so frightening; when we see him, a mild-mannered hotel clerk who could be anyone we pass on the street, we recognize the capacity for evil that exists within us and that we try so desperately to keep in check. Both religion and horror films teach us that we have to deal with the evil that exists within ourselves.

Monstrous Families

Many scholars have observed that the modern horror film forces us to rethink where the monster comes from. In the late 1960s, horror began depicting the family itself as monstrous, producing monstrous offspring. In *Rosemary's Baby* (1968), for example, Rosemary gradually realizes her husband and neighbors are involved in a terrifying plot to make sure she carries her baby to term; you see, Satan is actually the father, and the people that surround Rosemary are his servants. Whether intentional on the part of filmmakers or not, this new direction in horror emerged right as the nation was rethinking its relationship to authority in radical ways. While popular culture in the 1950s had extolled families like the one in *Leave It to Beaver*, by the end of the 1960s, Americans didn't have much trust in the family, the government, or any number of other institutions. Horror reflected that anxiety by showing the monstrous as emerging from within the family, producing violent, horrific offspring.

This theme is radically explored in Wes Craven's low-budget classic *The Hills Have Eyes* (1977). Before the director rose to fame on the back of Freddy Krueger, he made a couple of grindhouse pictures in the 1970s that have become horror standards, known mostly for their unflinching brutality. (The rape-revenge film *The Last House on the Left*, from 1972, is the other.) In some ways, *The Hills Have Eyes* fits into the "rural horror" cycle in which city dwellers are terrorized by unfriendly country folk.[1] The setup for *Hills* is conventional: a family is on a road trip to California, gets lost while trying to find a tourist destination in New Mexico, and has to fight for their lives against a clan of vicious hill people after their station wagon and trailer break down. Where it gets interesting is in the construction of each of these family units.

From the beginning, we learn that the extended Carter family is not exactly a harmonious unit. Patriarch Bob is a barely contained bundle of anger, ready to explode at any moment. We learn he's a retired police detective, but he doesn't seem to have liked his job much. He refers to having worked in the "worst precinct in Cleveland" and uses a racial epithet to refer to the people he supposedly served. During this tirade, it's easy to imagine him gleefully unloading pepper spray and tear gas on peaceful civil rights demonstrators. It doesn't seem like he was well regarded by his coworkers, either; without any explanation, he briefly mentions that he was shot at on two separate occasions by his own men.

This rant is but a preamble to Bob unloading on his wife, blaming her for landing their station wagon in a ditch (even though he was driving). "But none of these bastards ever came as close to killing me as my own goddamned wife and her goddamned road map," he snarls. His wife meekly responds, "Watch your language," as if his use of "goddamned" was the real problem with his monologue. Bob's method of taking charge is to immediately pull out his pistols, keeping one for himself and handing one to his teenage son, Bobby. As Bob walks off to find a gas station, he informs the family that "Bobby's in charge." In these few minutes of screen time, we're given a vivid portrait of Bob's misogyny and racism.

His wife seems to barely tolerate him, and his children don't think too highly of him either. Bob berates his wife and daughters and also subtly humiliates Bobby and Doug, his son-in-law. But Bob's not the only violent element in this clan. They have a nasty pair of German shepherds named Beauty and Beast who seem poised to attack anything that's not a part of the family. At one point, while Bob's wife and two daughters are waiting for him to return with help, they jokingly reminisce about an incident in Miami when Beast killed a poodle. They seem to have internalized that violence is part of how family systems work.

The horror of the film happens when the Carter family is attacked by their mirror image—a family who lives in the hills and preys on travelers who come through. After Bob dies in the initial attack, the two remaining Carter men are reduced to brutal means to defend the survivors; by the end of the movie, it's hard to tell the two groups apart. That's largely the point—the film suggests that the Carters are a slightly glossier version of this hill family and that both family units run on violence and domination. Scratch the surface of this smiling suburban family, and their meanness and brutality are revealed.

It's an unsettling film and not just because of the violence depicted on-screen. The deeper discomfort is in what it says about our own families and where monsters come from. The monstrous family from the hills are terrifying and cruel, no doubt. But the Carters don't appear much better. While most of their physical violence is perpetrated in self-defense, that doesn't account for how nasty they are to each other at the film's beginning. And it doesn't justify the film's final image of Doug viciously stabbing one of the antagonists over and over, continuing long after he's dead. Since rage-machine Bob has already met his demise and his son, Bobby, seems unable to pick up the mantle, the role of family patriarch has fallen to Doug. This unbridled violence is what being the family patriarch look like.

The hill family has one sympathetic member: abused daughter Ruby. When we first meet Ruby, she is trying to escape, hoping she can somehow find a normal life away from her family. This never comes to pass. But as her family kidnaps Doug and Lynne's baby, preparing to feast on it, Ruby's maternal instinct kicks in, and she attempts to rescue the child. In reaching toward something that looks like compassion, she's the only character who shows any kindness throughout the whole film. It's striking that the film ends with her screaming as she witnesses Doug's violence, almost as if she realizes that the problem isn't with her family but with the violence of the family system itself.

Herein lies the real discomfort of the film: its implication that families don't run on love and kindness but on tyranny and bloodshed. We don't get any easy, comfortable reassurance that the monster is outside of us in the struggle between good and evil. The film does not allow us to take for granted that we're on the side of good. When our own families become implicated in systems of domination, we begin to wonder if the monster isn't inside of us after all.

Religion and Identity

As a nation, America has a history of projecting the monstrous onto the Other. In many ways, this tendency can be traced back to the Puritans. They were a people filled with constant anxiety about whether the monstrous had crept into their community. Their attempts to locate the monstrous in the local indigenous tribes, or in witches who had infiltrated their towns, were evidence of a society that was unraveling.

The Puritan worldview was always full of tension. Good Puritans loved God, behaved in godly ways toward their neighbors, and kept their families on a holy path. And even more importantly, they did these things for the right reasons. If they were only outwardly good, but not conformed to God's will in their inward hearts, they were frauds, making a mockery of their religious convictions. It was a standard no one could possibly achieve. In this community, the price for claiming a Puritan identity was perpetual worry that you weren't living up to the expectations of your faith.

In short, the identity this religion gave was unstable, subject to change at any moment. Any misstep, any cross word to your neighbor or even a stray thought, and you were suddenly anathema. The Puritan community tried to pretend that the monsters were outside the colony walls—the Native Americans, the French settlers. But soon the monsters got closer, as they began to worry that monstrous witches were in their midst. Really, what they were worried about was that the monster was inside of them and that it had always been there.

This dynamic is dramatized perfectly in the 2015 film *The Witch*, which director Robert Eggers described as a "Puritan's nightmare." It follows a family who gets kicked out of the Massachusetts Bay Colony for oblique religious reasons—family patriarch William didn't agree with the colony's authorities and refused to recant his heretical beliefs—and sets up a homestead in the wilderness. After their infant goes missing, they begin to suspect that a witch is lurking in the wilderness. The suspicion then turns to their own eldest daughter, Thomasin, after her younger brother Caleb disappears in the woods and stumbles back home the next day at death's door. The suspicion the family casts on Thomasin proves to be a self-fulfilling prophecy.

If you've seen the film, you know that this brief summary doesn't begin to capture all its many twists. But even more important than these plot points are the complex relations within the family and the ways in which each member tries to live up to the ideals of their religion only to be wracked with guilt at constantly falling short. Pubescent Caleb can't seem to stop his eyes from lingering on his older sister's bosom, and Thomasin's prayers recount all the ways in which she has been disrespectful to her parents in her thoughts. William, the family patriarch, aspires to keep everyone on the straight and narrow like a good Puritan father, but he's prone to lying to take shortcuts to his desired ends. And his wife, Katherine, tries hard to be dutiful but can't completely suppress her desire for the comforts of life and for the home they left behind in England. It's a family of unhappy people, all of whom are pretending to be something they're not. They all believe that their identity has been given to them by their faith and by their family, and they desperately want to live into that identity. But it's not an ideal that fits.

Thomasin's plight is explored in the most depth. We see the shock on her face during the film's opening scene, when her father refuses to recant his beliefs in front of the Puritan tribunal, but the first time we hear her speak is in prayer. It's a private prayer of confession in which she bares her heart to God. And while she clearly feels a great deal of guilt over her behavior, the transgressions she describes don't rise to the level of severe offenses. "I've been idle of my work, disobedient of my parents, neglectful of my prayer," Thomasin laments. She continues, "I have, in secret, played upon thy Sabbath, and broken every one of thy commandments in thoughts." She can't shake her sense of guilt, and her guilt deepens throughout the film as she finds she can't do any better. She works so hard to be a compliant and faithful daughter, but she can't possibly live up to the expectations placed on her. As the family falls apart, Thomasin ends up in a pretty dreadful place.

While *The Witch* and *The Hills Have Eyes* are very different films—*The Witch* is a subtle piece of cinema, while *Hills* hits like a sledgehammer—they both make a similar point about the structure of the patriarchal family. In *Hills*, the family is run with cruel authoritarianism, victimizing nearly everyone. In *The Witch*, the ideals of the family place unreasonable burdens of self-sacrifice on each individual member, who buckle underneath their weight. *The Witch* also explores the burden of religious expectations. This element is only tangentially present in *Hills* through the figure of Bob's wife, who gathers the family together in prayer on several occasions and seems to take responsibility for their spiritual life. In *Hills*, religion is the domain of the feminine, twisted to give cover to the savagery displayed by the family's men. In *The Witch*, religion is another oppressive structure that combines with the institution of the family to create a set of impossible expectations. In neither story is religion an antidote to monstrosity.

Monsters aren't just scary creatures; they exist in stories, and they move and breathe in the narrative on the page or the screen. Descriptions of their appearance and their actions are part of the stories we tell about them around the campfire, during sleepovers, or in the newspapers. To be truly frightening, monsters can't just stand on the sidelines letting us gaze in awe at their terrifying construction. They have to be a part of a story to be truly frightening. They don't exist in a vacuum—they exist in the stories we tell about them.

In one of the earliest academic studies on monsters, Jeffrey Jerome Cohen suggested that "the monster always escapes."[2] On the literal level, we see this at the end of many horror movies, when the monster disappears to leave open the space for a sequel. But it also means that the monster doesn't stay where we put it. When we tell stories about the monster being outside—in the swamps, at Camp Crystal Lake, or anywhere else beyond the borders of our communities—the monster doesn't remain there. It creeps into our homes and crawls inside of us. And then we realize that the monster was there all along.

Religion often frankly acknowledges this truth. Paul was anguished about his inability to do the good that he wanted to do on account of the monstrous sin that existed inside himself. Acknowledging that we have this weakness is a good thing. Otherwise, we can spend our lives externalizing our own monstrosity: blaming others, looking for people to deport from the country, or punishing strangers in myriad ways. When we think the monster is only outside of ourselves, we detect the monster in all sorts of places and fail to realize it is thriving inside each and every one of us.

But if this realization is not accompanied by grace and understanding, our identification with the monster can easily lead to overwhelming feelings of guilt and shame. Paul's reflection on his state leads into his powerful discourse on grace in Romans 8; for Paul, the monster within can be overcome through this grace. But without grace, a focus on the monstrous self can leave people like Thomasin in *The Witch* weighed down by the anxiety of their internal struggles. *The Witch* is a powerful warning about the damage that religion can do when the knowledge of our sinful, monstrous natures isn't tempered with love.

We need stories that offer more nuanced views of the world beyond good and evil, us and the monster. Not only are good/evil dichotomies incomplete, as the family in *The Witch* learned, they're also tremendously fragile. Stories that account for the beautiful, and sometimes painful, messiness that actual life entails can withstand that challenge.

6

BEING FORGOTTEN, BEING REMEMBERED

PRECHAPTER VIEWING RECOMMENDATIONS

The Fog (John Carpenter, 1980)
Vanishing on 7th Street (Brad Anderson, 2010)

I n my work with Ecumenical Theological Seminary, I talk with pastors from all over the state of Michigan. Some of them lead thriving congregations that are making a difference in the lives of their members and their communities. But others manage struggling churches, churches that drift along from

Sunday to Sunday without really knowing what they're called to do. In many cases, these churches have a wonderful history, but they've fallen into the rut of declining membership, burned-out leaders, and an inability to stay relevant to a new generation. Too often, these churches decide that the best option they have is to live in the past. A pastor once stated one of the saddest things I've heard. "My congregation doesn't really want a pastor," he told me. "They want a museum curator."

The fear of being forgotten runs deep in these churches, as it does for many of us. This pastor's remark about being a "museum curator" struck at a deep and uncomfortable truth: rather than doing the hard work of remaining relevant to their community, which means speaking prophetically and making a difference for the people who walk through the doors, some churches have decided that the best they can do is raise the drawbridge and try to protect the memory of their past. I've seen many congregations where the median age of members is over sixty. For more than a few of those members, their primary attachment is that their parents or grandparents have their names on a plaque or a stained-glass window in the sanctuary. If the church goes bankrupt and closes its doors, there will be nothing left of that ancestor's memory.

The way we are remembered is important. We want people to recognize the work we do and admire us for it. It's why we give our names to bricks in the local park, submit obituaries to newspapers when our loved ones die, and put names on tombstones. It's at least partially why we have children. We want our stories to be told and remembered.

Both Jewish and Christian traditions, along with many others, place a high premium on memory. In each of these traditions, many rituals are centered on acts of remembering, whether it's Jews lighting a special candle on the first anniversary of the death of a loved one, or Christians' remembrance of Jesus's crucifixion on Good Friday. One of the foundational events of the Jewish faith, the Exodus, begins when the enslaved Jewish people cry out and God remembers them (Exodus 2:23–25). And in the New Testament, Jesus commands his followers to take communion in remembrance of him (Luke 22:19; 1 Corinthians 11:24–25).

These religious stories all circle around a vital truth: When we forget, we lose our way. When we remember, we at least have a chance.

In horror, the question of memory looms large as well. Frequently, the monster arrives because people have forgotten something important; they need to remember in order to make the evil go away. Particularly when the hidden knowledge is uncomfortable, the process of remembering what has been buried can be painful. But remembering it is a crucial part of what it means to be human.

RETURN OF THE REPRESSED

Sigmund Freud, the founder of psychoanalytic theory, used some of his ideas to understand works of literature, not just his patients. In his essay "The Uncanny," Freud asked what is behind the feelings of eeriness that are evoked by some works of literature. He spent a lot of time discussing E. T. A. Hoffmann's creepy story "The Sandman" (written in 1816), in which a man remembers a childhood fear about a figure who would sneak into children's bedrooms and steal their eyes. For Freud, the loss of eyes represents the fear of castration; that's not a route that many contemporary readers are willing to go down. But what's more interesting for me is Freud's next move. He says it's not that the fear of castration, in itself, is uncanny. What's uncanny is that this fear represents an earlier stage of development, one we thought we'd gone beyond. But now we find that it still has a hold on us. Robin Wood famously referred to this as "the return of the repressed," a motif Wood finds throughout the history of horror.

John Carpenter's film *The Fog* (1980) plays with these ideas in an interesting way. Instead of repression happening on the level of the individual, it encompasses an entire town. And what has been repressed is the truth of their history.

Unlike his earlier subgenre-defining slasher *Halloween*, Carpenter dialed back the violence and unspooled this as a slow-paced ghost story set in a Northern California fishing village. The initial cut of the film earned it only a mild PG rating. But in prerelease screenings, test audiences didn't respond well to it, which Carpenter chalked up to the recent release of gore-filled horror films such as *Phantasm* (1979). He went back and filmed an additional scene in which a group of seafarers is slaughtered in a visceral manner by the ghosts, which seemed to satisfy audiences. Rebranded as an adult, R-rated horror film, *The Fog* went on to do brisk business at the box office and secure Carpenter's status as a moneymaking director.

In *The Fog*'s opening sequence, a group of children are huddled together and fixated on a golden watch that is ticking loudly. When it snaps shut, the sea captain holding the watch pronounces to the children, "11:55. Almost midnight. Time for one more story." At midnight, it will be the one hundredth anniversary of a tragic event in the town's past when a clipper ship was lost in the fog. A light pierced through, promising the sailors safety, but instead of a lighthouse, it turned out to be a campfire, causing the ship to crash on the rocks. Someday, the captain tells the children, the fog will return, and the crew will rise from the sea, "in search of the campfire that led them to their dark, icy death." Of course, it is not lost on the children that they are huddled around a campfire themselves, making them a perfect target for the ghostly seafarers.

But as the fog returns the next morning, bringing the ghosts with it, it gradually becomes apparent that the campfire tale that opened the film didn't have all the details right. That's the story the townsfolk have told themselves for over a century, but it obscures the unsavory aspects of the town's origin: their community was founded by a band of wreckers who intentionally lured ships onto the rocks and plundered the valuables after the crew all drowned. The ghosts aren't coming back to find the campfire but to recover the treasure that was stolen from them, and to remind the town of its true history. In order for the town to be saved, the people have to remember.

It seems highly significant that this long-forgotten treasure has been buried in the walls of the village church. In fact, the crucifix over the church's altar was fashioned out of this ill-gotten booty—a rather heavy-handed metaphor for the myriad ways Christianity has sometimes built itself on a foundation of unethical behavior. But most interesting to me is the way *The Fog* presents the church as the receptacle of history for the town. Father Malone, the clergyman now in charge, isn't necessarily a bad person—in the film's climax, he puts the curse to rest with an act of self-sacrifice. But his grandfather, the previous town priest, was one of the six founders responsible for the original plunder and played a large part in keeping it all hidden. In *The Fog*, the only way the town could rewrite the story of its founding was with the complicity of the church, whose leaders concealed the real story.

In *The Fog*, the evil only dissipates when the villagers are able to acknowledge the truth of their past. It's a common pattern in ghost stories: the ghost brings something forgotten from the past, and the only way it can find peace is for us to remember. For us as well, the act of remembering is powerful. Sometimes, this can mean dredging up uncomfortable and unsavory parts of the past. Other times, it means holding on to pieces of the past that were good, even if the present doesn't seem to cohere with these truths.

There's no book of the Bible more concerned with memory than Deuteronomy, in which Moses (speaking on God's behalf) repeatedly calls for the people to remember. This pattern starts in the Ten Commandments, which contain an admonition to "remember that you were a slave in the land of Egypt, and the LORD your God brought you out from there with a mighty hand and an outstretched arm; therefore the LORD your God commanded you to keep the sabbath day" (Deuteronomy 5:15). The Sabbath is presented as a means of social justice; the people are supposed to have kindness toward their servants and even their livestock by giving them a break from work. They can keep this in the forefront of their mind by remembering how hard things were for them in Egypt, when they didn't have a Sabbath. By remembering what that was like, they'll always remember the importance of having a day of rest.

Deuteronomy offers other reasons to remember as well. When the long desert wanderings of the people of Israel are coming to an end and they are about the enter the promised land, Moses gives them a warning. "Remember the long way that the LORD your God has led you these forty years in the wilderness," he cautions (8:2), worried that they will take their blessings for granted and stray from the commandments of God. This advice still applies to us today. When we are prospering, remembering the hardships of the past can keep us grounded.

Throughout the Hebrew Bible/Old Testament, the people of Israel are told to remember that God brought them out of Egypt. It's a refrain when the armies of hostile nations are circling around, or when their temple is destroyed, or when they are driven into exile. *Remember that God delivered you before*, they are told. Because of this history, the people can find comfort in knowing that God will deliver them again. When God's people remember this, they can find the strength to get through the hard times in the present. In this case, remembering might not make the evil go away, but at least the monsters seem less menacing.

"I EXIST!"

Just as important as remembering is being remembered, a theme that is also common to both the biblical text and horror.

For those of us who believe that God knows all, the possibility that God could "forget" someone or something seems odd, even terrifying. It's an idea my seminary students push back on, objecting that "God knows everything; God can't forget." In more theological language, we want to believe God has "perfect knowledge," such that everything, past and present, is already known to God. But on many occasions, the Bible is clear that something has caused God to "remember" someone, and the only way God could remember is if God had forgotten.

The Bible's early books contain a prime example of this, offering insight into how, for the biblical authors, God's memory might work. In Genesis, God makes a covenant with Abraham, promising that his descendants will be more numerous than the sands of the sea and that they will inherit the land of Canaan (Genesis 12:7; 22:17–18). But Exodus, the next book in the Bible, begins several generations after Abraham, and the situation has changed. Now, the people of Israel are slaves in Egypt, being pressed into hard labor to support Pharaoh's building projects. "The Israelites groaned under their slavery, and cried out for help," the text reads (2:23). When these cries reach God, God hears them and "remember[s] his covenant with Abraham" (2:24). God decides to help the people.

In Exodus, the experience of being, or at least feeling, forgotten by God occurs on the level of the community. It is the people of Israel God is remembering. But in the psalms, this experience of feeling forgotten by God becomes much more personal. Psalm 13 begins with the plaintive cry, "How long, O Lord? Will you forget me forever?" And Psalm 88, quite possibly the bleakest of all psalms, finds the speaker lamenting that he is "like those forsaken among the dead, like the slain that lie in the grave, like those whom you remember no more, for they are cut off from your hand" (88:4). Here, the psalmist fears being cast into the shadowy realm of Sheol, the place where the dead go to be forgotten. While other scriptures suggest that God does, in fact, maintain power over the dead in Sheol, the author of Psalm 88 seems convinced otherwise. This is the only psalm that ends on a note of despair, without the psalmist expressing confidence that God will offer deliverance in the end.

There are also psalms where the entire community laments together, and these likewise express the dread of being forgotten by God. While Psalm 9:12 affirms that God "does not forget the cry of the afflicted," the communal lament of Psalm 44 puts this to question: "Why do you hide your face? Why do you forget our affliction and oppression?" (v. 24). This community has heard of the great deeds God did for their ancestors (v. 1), but their present experience is one of abandonment. "Rise up, come to our help," the psalm concludes. "Redeem us for the sake of your steadfast love" (v. 26). These writers can only hold on to the stories of God's saving actions among their ancestors and hope those actions will be repeated in the present day.

Whether or not God can forget is a rather abstract theological question. In some ways, it seems almost like a moot point; I don't know enough to give an answer, and my opinion on the matter doesn't affect the reality one way or another. However, the *experience* of feeling forgotten by God is real, as attested by many of the biblical authors.

It's also attested in horror films. While *The Fog* explored the importance of remembering and of being faithful to the sometimes uncomfortable truths of the past, the 2010 film *Vanishing on 7th Street*, directed by Brad Anderson, addresses the fear of being forgotten as an individual. Anderson has worked in a wide range of genres from comedy to action, but horror seems to be his preferred mode. His film *Session 9* (2001), an eerie, slow burn of a movie about a group of workers hired to remove the asbestos from an abandoned mental institution, has become an underground classic among horror fans. More recently, his Netflix original film *Fractured* (2019) follows a father who takes his daughter to the emergency room, only to discover the next day that none of the hospital staff has any recollection of her. In some ways, these are both better films than *Vanishing on 7th Street*; the acting is stronger, the scripts tighter, and the themes more coherent. But there's a haunting quality about *Vanishing* that left me unable to shake it after seeing it soon after its release, and its themes are deeply relevant to this chapter.

In somewhat of a forerunner to *Bird Box* (2018), *Vanishing* addresses what it means to remain behind. In the film's opening, the lights suddenly go off everywhere; when they come back on, the only thing left of most people is a pile of empty clothing to mark where they had been. The film's protagonists are only saved because each of them was somehow in contact with a light source that didn't depend on the electrical grid, holding a flashlight or near a candle for example. They were saved by the light.

The film's opening scene is set in a multiplex movie theater as a crowd is enjoying the latest popcorn flick. The sequence follows Paul, who is working in the projection room. Suddenly, everything goes dark except for the headlamp he is wearing, and the film stops. Paul runs to the projector to see what the matter is, but before he can figure it out, the lights have returned and the film has resumed. But the audience is gone—they're simply piles of clothes clustered in the now-empty seats. One moment, the filmgoers were living and enjoying the world; then suddenly they weren't.

Neither is the threat contained after that initial attack. As the sunlight grows shorter each day, the edges around the light become populated with vaguely human-shaped shadows, bending around the bright edges and waiting for the light to recede. If anyone steps outside of the light, these shadows are ready to pounce. They smother their victims, leaving only their clothes behind. It's like the victims never existed; they've been utterly forgotten.

In the film, we follow a group of survivors holed up in a downtown Detroit bar, waiting in dread for the inevitable moment when their generator will fail and the lights will be extinguished. Their desperate need to reaffirm their existence in the face of impending nothingness is the major driver of the film. It's what keeps the characters going, refueling the bar's backup generator to sustain the lights just a little longer. This is first articulated by Luke (Hayden Christensen, in a performance only slightly less cringe-inducing than his turn as Anakin Skywalker), who feels the only way he can stave off the shadows is to keep reminding himself, "I exist." It becomes a mantra of sorts for the characters throughout the film; as Paul the projectionist meets his end, surrounded by hungry shadows, he keeps repeating the phrase until there is nothing left of him to struggle. In a chilling detail, after another character has met a horrible demise, the surrounding shadows seem to be echoing this plea, either in mockery or unthinking imitation of their human prey.

The moral center of the film is young Jesse, a twelve-year-old boy whose mother works at the bar. She heard there were lights on at the church down the block and went to check them out; now, days later, Jesse is still convinced that she will return. As the lights start to disappear at the bar, he makes a mad dash for the church, aided by some rather silly plot devices. The only lights he finds are a group of candles burning around the altar, so he runs down the aisle toward them, just out of the clutches of the reaching shadows, and lies down with the candles surrounding him. He crosses his arms over himself, repeating, "I exist," as the candles fade one by one. Finally, there's only one left—but miraculously, it lasts until the sunrise. The scene recalls the miracle of Hanukkah, commemorating a time in the second century BCE when Jewish revolutionaries who retook their temple had enough oil to keep their candles burning for a single night, but instead, the candles miraculously burned for eight. Although religious iconography is not strong through the majority of *Vanishing*, it becomes almost overwhelming in this scene, as the camera cuts to the flickering light on the statues of Christ and other saints lining the front of the church. Jesse has found his sacred space, and it confirms that he does, indeed, exist. While we don't know how long Jesse will continue to survive—the film ends before the next night comes—the burning candle of this scene evokes the possibility that God has remembered Jesse.

BEING FORGOTTEN

Vanishing on 7th Street, while far from a perfect film, dramatizes the deep insight that asserting our existence is the only weapon we have against nothingness. When the film's characters are threatened by the consuming shadows, their only hope is to blindly hold on to the reality of their existence for as long as they can. It's a struggle against annihilation, a refusal to "go gentle into that good night,"[1] and an assertion that, by holding on to our existence, we can forestall this descent into nothingness.

The poet of Psalm 88, who fears being dragged down into Sheol, is engaged in this same struggle. Frequently, Sheol is portrayed like these voracious shadows of *Vanishing on 7th Street*, a cavernous, yawning mouth that threatens to erase anything it can swallow. In Numbers, set during the time when the Israelites are wandering in the wilderness between Egypt and Canaan, some priests led by the Levite Korah rebel against Moses's authority. They want to assert that Moses has no special powers over them, that each of these priests (and, indeed, everyone) can be just as close to God as Moses is. "All the congregation are holy," they say to Moses.

I can empathize with their claim, as I'm sure many of us can. We want to be special. We want to have it recognized that we have the same gifts as anyone else. In some ways, this is its own struggle against being forgotten—these Levites didn't want to be overshadowed by Moses, but to be recognized as great men. (Yes, they were all men.) But this isn't the way to go about being remembered. They're remembered as a part of our religious heritage (at least, for the brave few who wander into the book of Numbers), but they're remembered for stubbornly trying to rewrite their place in history rather than giving an honest telling of their own story. Moses proposes a test: if these rebellious Levites live their lives as normal, without any consequences, then they are speaking the truth. But the people can know that they are in the wrong if "the ground opens its mouth and swallows them, and they go down alive into Sheol" (Numbers 16:30). Sure enough, a few verses later, "the earth opened its mouth and swallowed them" (16:33). And not just them, but their entire households and everything they own. They vanish without a trace, swallowed whole by the underworld.

No museum marks their possessions, and they leave nothing behind for future generations to remember them except for the story of how they vanished.

That's not how we want to be remembered. So we struggle against the shadows, remembering where we've been through the rituals we reenact every year and every week, and telling our story in a way that others will remember it. And we hope that we can be brave enough to have the true story of our lives be told, rather than have it buried in the church walls. If our story is buried, we might as well have been swallowed alive by the shadows or by Sheol.

These twin struggles—to remember and to be remembered—are a deep part of what it means to be human. Memory is what connects us to our ancestors and our descendants, the past and the future. Without memory, we're disconnected individuals, our lives bounded by our births and our deaths. The acts of remembering and being remembered prompt us to look outside of our own lives for meaning, finding a picture that's bigger than ourselves.

7

FAIR'S FAIR

Creepshow (George Romero, 1982)
Tales from the Crypt (HBO series; various
directors, 1989–1996)

I'm pretty sure my oldest child didn't emerge from the womb with a fully developed sense of the concept of fairness, but by the time their younger sibling was born, they had a finely attuned antenna for anything that felt like injustice. The younger sibling has also acquired this profound need for there to be not even a whiff of favoritism in the family. When I recently stopped at a fast-food drive-through window with my oldest as a treat when they were sick, the first thing the little brother yelled was "No fair!" before stopping to consider for a minute. Then he responded, thoughtfully, "Last week, when Dad and I went fishing together, he got me a candy bar." The two siblings smiled at each other, complicit in their knowledge that each of them had recently been the beneficiary of an unfair treat. The scales were balanced, and all was right in their small corners of the world.

We all have this need for fairness, this desire to see things even out—at least as far as our own experiences are concerned. It's harder to develop the same drive for fair outcomes for others, but it's something most of us try to work on as we grow into adulthood. We want to experience the world as being a fundamentally fair place where people get rewarded for good actions. And we want to believe that when bad things happen (at least to other people), their misfortunes are the result of poor choices, in one way or another.

While we know the world is frustratingly more complicated than that, the instinct for fairness is deeply rooted and can even override other drives. A research study known as the "Ultimatum Game" demonstrates how important this concept is to many people.[1] This simple experiment starts with two people. One is randomly selected to receive ten dollars (or more, depending on how and when the experiment was run). This person, known as "the proposer," gets to decide how to divide this money between themselves and the other person, "the responder." The catch is that if the responder doesn't agree to the proposal, both participants walk away with nothing. Frequently, the proposer will offer something like a 60-40 split— the other person still gets something, so it doesn't make sense to turn it down, right? Wrong. If the responder doesn't perceive the deal being proposed as fair, they'll reject it, leaving both parties unhappy. As economist Bart Wilson explains it, the people involved don't "care about what is optimal; they care about what is fair." And while Wilson notes that many languages don't have a single word that can be precisely translatable as "fair," most cultures understand the concept deeply.

Sociologist Arlie Russell Hochschild's fascinating book *Strangers in Their Own Land* explores the political identities of communities in the rural South, but it also functions as an extended meditation on how people can understand the concept of fairness in different ways. For many of the (mostly white) people she interviewed, Hochschild found "waiting in line" as being a key image through which their experience of the world is filtered. "The sun is hot and the line unmoving," as Hochschild tells the story. "In fact, is it moving backward? You haven't gotten a raise in years, and there is no talk of one."[2] But there are other people who seem to be cutting in line—"You're following the rules. They aren't." This is a story about the fundamental fairness of the world, and the ways in which people perceive our government to be working for or against that sense of fairness. In interview after interview, Hochschild listens to people talking about affirmative action, gender equality programs, and government-supported access to health care as ways for the government to help people cut in line. If we perceive a government program as being unfair in how it distributes benefits, we're not going to support it no matter how much good it might do. Even if we have to give up the four dollars we've been offered, we're not going to let the other party walk away with six.

One of the reasons people are drawn to religion is for the promise of a world that's structured fairly. If we can believe in a God who rewards the righteous and punishes the wicked, then we can hold out hope that things will be made right—if not in this life, then surely in the world to come. Often, belief in God goes hand in hand with a belief, or at least a wish, that the world is fair and that if we do the right thing and live our lives faithfully, we'll be rewarded.

This fixation on fairness is another strange overlap between religion and horror. Despite how transgressive horror can be, much of it is also deeply invested in a worldview in which wicked people get punished for doing deplorable things, preferably in ways that contain a heavy dose of literary irony. We'll explore how this works in the old EC Comics like *Tales from the Crypt*, as well as modern incarnations of these stories such as the film *Creepshow* (1982). Although horror and religion are clearly different in their modes of expression, both envision a world where fairness rules overall.

DEEDS AND CONSEQUENCES IN THE BIBLE

As an example of Bart Wilson's idea that there's not a precise equivalent for the term *fair* in some non-English languages, the Bible has a few ways it describes this concept. In the Hebrew Bible/Old Testament, the closest equivalent might be *tzedek* ("righteous" or maybe "just"); often, when a verdict or an agreement is thought to be fair, the Hebrew word *tov* ("good") is how it is described. Similarly, the New Testament uses Greek words like *isos* ("equal" or "the same") or *kalos* ("good"). And while what it means for something to be "fair" in these contexts might be somewhat different from how we understand it in twenty-first-century America, there's clearly a value placed on equity, some sense of fairness.

Deuteronomy is Moses's farewell speech to the people of Israel, given as they stand on the precipice of entering the promised land of Canaan (a land Moses will not be allowed to enter himself). Near the end of this speech, after a lengthy list of dos and don'ts for the people, Moses gives a clear definition of what "fair" meant to the ancient Israelites. "If you obey the commandments of the LORD your God that I am commanding you today," Moses tells them, "by loving the LORD your God, walking in his ways, and observing his commandments, decrees, and ordinances, then you shall live and become numerous, and the LORD your God will bless you in the land that you are entering to possess" (Deuteronomy 30:16). It's a simple idea: if the people do well, behaving the way God has asked them to, they'll receive the gifts of good, long lives, with many descendants to carry on their stories after they're gone. In the next breath, Moses gives the reverse of this: if they don't follow the commandments, they'll lead short, miserable lives.

This is what fairness means in Deuteronomy: an if-then equation that those who follow the rules will be rewarded and those who do not will be punished. A similar idea permeates Proverbs, also in the Hebrew Bible/Old Testament. Proverbs is part of the Wisdom Tradition, a group of books—also including Ecclesiastes and Job, as well as Sirach and the Wisdom of Solomon in some traditions—that focus on ethical training. They're frequently framed as being instruction from a wise individual to a student, sometimes as advice from father to son. While the most famous examples are preserved in the Bible, these books bear close resemblance to works from Egypt, Mesopotamia, and other nations of ancient times. More than any other part of the Bible, the Wisdom Tradition is cosmopolitan.

In Proverbs, the instructor frequently offers two possible ways of living, with two possible outcomes. Near the book's beginning, Dame Wisdom promises that "waywardness kills the simple, and the complacency of fools destroys them; but those who listen to me will be secure and will live at ease, without dread of disaster" (Proverbs 1:32–33). Some of the two-line maxims that fill the book are even clearer: "The house of the wicked is destroyed, but the tent of the upright flourishes" (Proverbs 14:11). Or, "The way of the lazy is overgrown with thorns, but the path of the upright is a level highway" (Proverbs 15:19). The point of all these maxims is clear. If you live the right way, you'll achieve a prosperous and happy outcome. If you're wicked, lazy, or foolish, you can expect disaster. For Proverbs, this is what constitutes fairness: everyone getting what they deserve.

It's an appealing idea, and it's comforting to think that the world might work this way. Except that it doesn't. We can all think of times when we've done the right thing and weren't repaid in the way we felt we should have been. Maybe there was a project at work for which you weren't recognized or even where someone else took the credit. Or maybe you studied hard for a test but still didn't do well. And on the larger scale, we can all think of people who behave unethically and do not seem to be punished for it. Businesspeople take advantage of their employees, people don't treat their spouses well, and some people slide through life without putting in any real effort but always seem to fall into the right places. We know that life doesn't really pass out rewards and punishments based on some predictable measure of fairness.

What's astonishing is that the Bible knows this too. The Hebrew Bible/Old Testament doesn't have a developed idea of life after death—the closest we get to an afterlife is the remembrance of our name that endures through our children. Many scholars posit that the idea of life after death in the Jewish tradition arose later, during the Hellenistic period, an era when Jews were experiencing increasingly harsh treatment at the hands of political authorities and increasingly less autonomy. As life became brutal and arbitrary, ideas of the afterlife developed—the ultimate leveler of the field. If the faithful are receiving cruel treatment in this life, the Bible began to say, the scales will all be balanced in the world to come. But for much of the period when the Hebrew Bible/Old Testament was being written, there was a palpable frustration at the lack of fairness during this earthly existence.

One of the clearest examples of this grievance is in Job, another book from the Wisdom Tradition. In this book, Job is an exemplary person: he's fair in his dealings, he's raising an impressive family, and everyone seems to love him. He's been rewarded with a huge estate and the respect of his community. But one day, it all falls apart. Some of Job's livestock are burned in a fire; others carried off by raiders. His servants are killed.

While Job is still processing this news, he learns that his children died when their house collapsed on them. Eventually, he winds up with sores and boils covering his skin, sitting on the garbage heap at the edge of town, wondering why God allowed this to happen. (The readers know, troublingly, that it's because God and Satan made a bet about Job's faith and integrity, so Satan has been permitted to visit all these calamities on Job as a perverse test. Job never learns of this behind-the-scenes wager.)

Much of the book is recounted in the form of a series of speeches between Job and the three friends who begin by consoling him but soon start arguing with him. They offer several rationales for why these terrible misfortunes have befallen Job. Perhaps he's sinned in some way and is being punished for it. Or perhaps he's being tested, and he'll be rewarded eventually. But Job is steadfast—if he's done something wrong, he wants to know what it is. If no one can tell him that, he wants to make his case directly to God. For Job, this is a question of the fundamental fairness of the universe.

Job's appeal to God is granted, in that he gets an audience of sorts with the deity. However, Job doesn't receive the straight answer he's been hoping for. Instead, God chides him for thinking too much of himself. "Where were you when I laid the foundation of the earth?" God demands. "Tell me, if you have understanding" (Job 38:3). God proceeds to take Job to task by focusing on all the places that exist—and even thrive—without humanity. God points out that rain falls "on a land where no one lives" (Job 38:26). This tour ends with the majestic and terrifying beasts of Behemoth and Leviathan, creatures that are powerful forces of destruction but nevertheless have a place in the universe. It's a picture of a world that's far outside of Job's control, one he can hardly fathom. It's worth pointing out that the Hebrew text of Job starts out very simply—the first chapter is something that my Hebrew students can read without much trouble in the middle of their first year of studying the language. But the poetry of God's speech in the culmination of the book is some of the most difficult Hebrew in the entire Bible, filled with complex grammatical structures and obscure vocabulary. This poet used every tool available to describe the sublime.

What does this all have to do with fairness? It's a question that has baffled interpreters for millennia. The best I can offer is that this vision of a cosmos that's so much larger than Job has imagined is intended to convey the message that his idea of fairness is far too small. The simple system of rewards and punishments he has envisioned doesn't begin to encapsulate all the mysteries and wonders of the universe. But then the book pulls a final twist; after this dressing-down that Job receives from God, he walks back into his life to find that he's been granted new wealth and new children. The fairy-tale ending is clearly another subversion, causing us to ask whether there is something to this idea of rewards and punishments after all. Maybe the universe is far more complicated than we understand. Job learned that the universe operates on a logic that is far different from that of any human conceptions of fairness. But then he gets rewarded for his righteousness anyway, just as if the universe did operate on such simplistic concepts. So perhaps there is a beating heart of fairness underneath all the sublime mystery, one that we can yearn for even when it seems elusive and even when our experience tells us that it's not so.

A DIME'S WORTH OF HORROR

In the 1950s, comic books were just beginning to reach into the minds of young readers across the world. Some of our most well-known superheroes were already in place; Superman made his first appearance in 1938 (in *Action Comics #1*), with Batman following a year later (*Detective Comics #27*). But many others wouldn't come along until the early 1960s, when the fledgling company Marvel Comics introduced us to Spider-Man (*Amazing Fantasy #15*, 1962) and the X-Men (*X-Men #1*, 1963). As superhero comics were just getting off the ground, pages were also filled every month with detective stories, cowboy yarns, and grim portrayals of war. Perhaps no comics of this era left a stronger mark on American culture than the horror genre that made its way onto drugstore racks in the 1950s.

Entertaining Comics (most commonly known just as EC) was producing a handful of wholesome titles for young readers when William Gaines inherited the company after his father's death in 1947. The younger Gaines pushed the company in a decidedly darker direction, launching a line of titles for more mature readers. Most famous of these were the horror comics, including *Tales from the Crypt*, *The Vault of Horror*, and *The Haunt of Fear*. These stories featured all manner of murder, mayhem, and nastiness. They were graphic enough that they launched congressional hearings and state-level attempts to ban them across the country.[3] The end result was the creation of the Comics Code Authority, an attempt by the comic book industry to police itself so Congress wouldn't intervene. From the mid-1950s, almost every comic carried the seal of approval from the Comics Code Authority until the system fell apart in the mid-1980s. But if the censors had bothered to look beyond the blood and gore, they would have found a worldview that was actually quite conservative. Like in the Wisdom Tradition of the Bible, bad people in these comics needed to be punished.

Perhaps the most notorious story, and one that was discussed quite a bit at the congressional hearings, was a nasty little piece called "Foul Play," written and illustrated by Al Feldstein and Jack Davis. (It originally appeared in *Haunt of Fear* #*19*, 1953.) When a Bayville baseball player dies in the middle of a game, his team realizes he had been poisoned with one of their opponent's cleats. After the game, they lure the murderer back to the baseball stadium; not content to simply kill him, the story ends with the Bayville team playing a game with this unfortunate player's body parts—using his severed leg as a bat, pitching with his head, having his heart stand in for home plate, and lining the base paths with his intestines. It's almost hilariously grim, far beyond the realm of anything like good taste. This gallows humor was reinforced by the frame stories, in which a ghoulish host introduces and sums up each narrative. The most famous was the Crypt Keeper, who was resurrected by HBO years later. He ends "Foul Play" by warning the readers to watch where they sit the next time they attend a

Bayville game: "That night, one of Bayville's boys hit a homer, into the stands. They never found the . . . heh, heh . . . 'ball'!" Along with the over-the-top gore and groan-inducing puns, "Foul Play" demonstrates horror comics' fixation with payback in the form of poetic justice.

Another great example of this is in "Split Personality," from *Haunt of Fear #29* (1955), in which a small-time con man gets greedy when he learns of the existence of two wealthy, neurotic twin sisters. He figures he can double his payout if he pretends to have a twin brother himself and marries both sisters. Unfortunately for him, the women figure this out and decide that the only fair thing to do is split him down the middle. Literally.

While a vengeful plot is a common pattern in these classic comics, it can easily be found in other areas of horror as well. Many of the best-known *Twilight Zone* television episodes from the 1950s are built on this idea, as are the slasher films of the 1980s. Most of the segments of George A. Romero's *Creepshow*, a 1982 film based on short stories from Stephen King, also follow this logic. Robin Wood dismissed *Creepshow* as "nasty people doing nasty things to other nasty people," but he seems to have missed the connection with the moral worldview of the EC Comics tradition.[4] Both *Creepshow* and *Creepshow 2* (1987) are built around framing stories that feature comics, which are obviously modeled after the classic EC series. The sequel's first segment, "Old Chief Wood'nhead," is problematic on multiple political levels, with stereotypes flying. But the logic of deeds-consequences provides a clear structuring pattern. A cigar store statue of an Indian comes to life to take revenge after the owner of his shop is murdered by a gang of robber-murderers that is led by a Native American man. Because this man dreams of leaving his reservation for Hollywood and has forgotten his heritage, the film seems to imply, his heritage comes back to kill him in the form of the statue, come to life as a Native American warrior. Everyone is sorted neatly into categories of good and bad, and bad people have to be punished for their misdeeds.

In the final segment, "The Hitchhiker," a woman runs over a man on the side of the road, but he returns to haunt her in increasingly threatening ways. To emphasize that this is her payback for running him over, he keeps repeating the mantra, "Thanks for the ride, lady!" Her sins are clearly established from the outset—the late-night drive she's undertaking is the result of having spent the evening with another man and racing to get home before her hardworking husband arrives back. She compounds this sin by believing she can ignore the man she ran over, telling herself that it's more important to reach home ahead of her husband. Sin compounds sin, and before she knows it, she's got a bloody zombie hitchhiker in the front seat with her. The gender ideology at play here is particularly regressive; while evildoers of all kinds get their comeuppances in horror, it seems like special punishments are reserved for unfaithful women.

Since then, the formula has been repeated most clearly in HBO's *Tales from the Crypt* series, which ran on the network from 1989 to 1996. Each episode was based on an EC Comics story and featured a puppet Crypt Keeper as the host and dispenser of terrible jokes. There were even a couple of (poorly received) spin-off theatrical films: *Tales from the Crypt Presents: Demon Knight* (1995) and *Tales from the Crypt Presents: Bordello of Blood* (1996). But the late-night series definitely captured the spirit of EC. Many of the episodes revolved around the same simple crime-and-punishment formula. There were stories about a robber whose conscience wouldn't stop talking to him, even after he ended up in prison ("For Cryin' Out Loud," in which loudmouthed comedian Sam Kinison plays the doomed man's conscience); a man who gives a love potion to a beautiful woman, only to realize that he can't get rid of her afterward ("Loved to Death"); and a sleazy salesman who knocks on the wrong door and finds himself in the clutches of a terrifying family—each member played by Tim Curry ("Death of Some Salesman"). There's also an adaptation of "Split Personality" with Joe Pesci in the role of the con man trying to marry twin sisters. This series was hugely influential in my development as a horror fan. In my high school years, I'd frequently record each new episode on Friday night and then wait until my parents were gone to watch it. In one of my best memories from high school, my parents left for a weekend fishing trip, leaving me home alone for an overnight that happened to coincide with a *Tales from the Crypt* marathon on HBO. Rather than inviting friends over for a party, I made a cannister of Pillsbury cinnamon rolls and proceeded to eat the entire batch while the mayhem played out on the living room screen.

The EC Comics formula is brilliant, offering the reader or viewer enjoyment on multiple levels. For many, the grisly (and highly creative!) violence is itself a draw—as we discussed in chapter 4, horror's ability to demonstrate the myriad ways in which our bodies are vulnerable has the power to enthrall. If the gore starts to be a little too much, the humor undercuts it, allowing the tale to exploit the thin line between horror and laughter. Underneath this, there's something reassuring about the moral universe the formula depicts—a universe where nasty things happen to bad people. The corollary of this is that if nasty things happen to bad people, then good things must happen to virtuous, upstanding people. It's the world that Proverbs describes, and which Job desperately wants to believe in.

It's one that still speaks to us today. When we encounter life's unfairness, we experience powerlessness. If you had the power to make things right, you would—but for whatever reason, you don't have that power. It might be because you're ten, and you can't drive yourself to McDonald's to make up for the lunch your older sibling got. Or it might be that our capitalist system is rigged to favor those who already have wealth and power and that it's been built to favor continued accumulation by the few. On varying levels, from the minute to the profound, we all experience these injustices every day—when we go to work, when we pay our taxes, when we try to figure out how we're going to help our kids go to college. And that's just from my perspective as a straight white male.

We like to think that there's something at work under this structure, some benevolent force that's trying to put the scales back into balance. The systems that run our communities and our country might not be fair, but part of us hopes for universal laws to ensure that those of us who live righteously get rewarded and those who do evil get what's coming to them. Such a world-view may be simplistic, but it has a powerful draw. It's easy to see how it can go wrong, particularly when ham-handed theologians like Pat Robertson or Jerry Falwell proclaim that 9/11 was the fault of the LGBTQ+ community, feminists, and abortion providers or that Hurricane Katrina was judgment on New Orleans for Mardi Gras.[5] These kinds of ridiculous and hurtful statements make the limitations of this worldview painfully apparent.

In Christianity, the theology that has taken this worldview to its logical extreme is known as the Prosperity Gospel, an uncomfortable blend of Proverbs' maxims of rewards and punishments with a Norman Vincent Peale–style emphasis on the power of positive thinking. Prosperity theology teaches that God is always looking to reward the faithful, which happens through material blessings. For God to know you're faithful, you need to make a financial investment in the work of His (always His, in the language of prosperity preachers) Kingdom. Those who make that financial investment will be awarded material blessings like money and a nice car.

This theology is crap. Even in its strictest biblical form, the promises of deeds-consequences don't lay out exactly what a faithful believer should expect to receive. Psalm 1 tells us that the person who meditates on the instructions of God day and night will be "happy," or maybe "blessed" (depending on how you want to translate the Hebrew *makerah*), but it doesn't fully articulate what a blessed state looks like. It seems to entail a confidence, a sense of being right with the world, as you rest easily with the knowledge that you're living a good life. That may or may not happen while you've got a new Mercedes parked in your driveway. When preachers get specific about what a blessing from God should look like, I start looking for the exit.

That's because promises of material wealth for the faithful can also be damaging. What does it say to the faithful church member who donates all she can, gives of her time to serve others, and still needs help to make ends meet each month? Is her lack of financial security because her faith isn't strong enough, she isn't praying loud enough, or she isn't good enough? If we believe that God rewards the faithful with material blessings, that woman's situation leaves us with only two conclusions—either God isn't holding up God's end of the bargain, or the church member is doing something wrong to not deserve those financial blessings. We're stuck in the position of Job's friends, telling him that he must have done something wrong to deserve the treatment he got from God.

It's a tough conundrum. And it's one many of us struggle with on an individual level, every day. I'm sure a big part of the reason I was so drawn to HBO's *Tales from the Crypt* was that it gave me hope in my own little high school world; maybe the kids who looked down on me, who seemed to rule the world and have it all, weren't always going to be top dogs. It's not that I wished for a zombie hitchhiker to come after them, at least not most of the time, but I held out hope that I would one day see them reap the consequences of their shallow, mean-spirited existences. As

I've grown, I try to worry less about what others get, but it's hard not to make those comparisons. Sometimes, we just want to imagine that things will be fair, someday soon.

I don't believe in a God who strikes some people with illness or poverty. Right now, I try to hold on to faith in a God who is grieving along with the world and works in subtle ways to spur us into action. I'm grateful for my blessings and recognize that many of them are undeserved. Sometimes, the world just works that way.

8

FIGHT THE POWER

The Purge (James DeMonaco, 2013)
Us (Jordan Peele, 2019)

In the last chapter, we explored concepts of fairness, and how this desire plays out in our day-to-day lives. In this chapter, we'll turn our attention to the related concept of justice. If fairness is something you experience personally, justice has to do with the structures of society. Justice is fairness writ large. However, that doesn't mean that individuals don't feel the absence of justice inscribed into their bodies. While the problem is systemic, the results are focused on individuals.

I grew up in East Lansing, the home of Michigan State University, and my family were faithful members of Edgewood

United Church. I knew from an early age that the church's commitment to social justice was one of the things that drew my parents to it; the church's founding pastor, Truman Morrison, was deeply involved in the push for integrated housing in the city. What I didn't find out until much later was that the city didn't allow people of color to rent or buy homes until 1968.[1] This isn't ancient history—it's only eight years before I was born.

In my privileged state, it didn't occur to me that these kinds of discriminatory housing practices have repercussions long beyond their expiration date (even if we were to assume that discriminatory housing practices have ended, which study after study shows they haven't). As Ta-Nehisi Coates profoundly explored in his essay "The Case for Reparations," housing policies not only circumscribe where people live but also confine their ability to build wealth.[2] For many white families, the wealth they built to help their children succeed in life was the direct result of the home they owned. Black families were systematically excluded from this means of wealth-building for generations, an impact that continues to be felt.

Religion's role is to unmask injustice, imagine a better world, and provide tools to make that world a reality. But in another interesting reflection, horror performs the same functions. Often, horror takes pieces of the injustice of our world and literalizes them in some way, or pushes them to an extreme to make the injustice clear and obvious. *The Purge* universe and Jordan Peele's film *Us* (2019) have both worked to expose the unjust systems of our world.

Social Justice in the Bible and Religious Tradition

Social justice lies at the heart of the Jewish and Christian traditions, and that emphasis begins with the Hebrew Bible. In Deuteronomy 10:17–18, for example, the Israelites' God is described as one who secures justice for the widow, the orphan, and the foreigner. And although Leviticus is often thought of as a dry book of rituals (a view that's not completely unfounded), the final chapters have a strong focus on social justice. Leviticus 19:18 famously admonishes the people to "love your neighbor as yourself," a saying that is familiar to many Christians because Jesus quotes it in the New Testament. Leviticus 25 then introduces the idea of Jubilee, the practice of forgiving all debts every fifty years. While it's easy to find flaws in these commandments—the Jubilee regulations are only meant to govern relations between Israelites, for example—the overall thrust is clear. Social justice is at the center of the law.

Justice takes an even more prominent place in the writings of the prophets, such as Jeremiah, Amos, and Isaiah. While many people today think of a prophet as someone who predicts the future, like the predictions of Nostradamus that show up every year in supermarket tabloids, the Bible treats them differently. In the Bible's prophetic books, a prophet is someone who speaks on behalf of God, and who—through this relationship—has a unique insight into the realities of the current situation. They're less about foretelling than they are about truth telling.

Even when prophets do tell the future, most often it isn't in the form of a prediction, but a factual statement about where the people's actions are going to lead them. In many cases, the prophets follow the deeds-consequences worldview we talked about in the last chapter. As God has Jeremiah tell the people, "Your ways and your doings have brought this upon you" (Jeremiah 4:18).

The prophets' critiques of their societies are wide-ranging: they are worshipping other gods, allying with foreign governments, and burning incense that God says is a stinky abomination (Isaiah 1:13). But they continually circle back to questions of greed, exploitation, and lack of fairness in the judicial system. In a lengthy diatribe outlining the sins of the people, God says to Jeremiah, "For scoundrels are found among my people; they take over the goods of others . . . their houses are full of treachery; therefore they have become great and rich, they have grown fat and sleek" (Jeremiah 5:26–27). To amplify these wrongdoings, the powerful use the judicial system to further ensconce their wealth and privilege: "They know no limits in deeds of wickedness; they do not judge with justice the cause of the orphan, to make it prosper, and they do not defend the rights of the needy" (Jeremiah 5:28). The verdict is clear. While the people's sins are many, doing injustice to their neighbors is at the heart of their crimes.

The book of Amos is equally clear about how much God wants the people to practice social justice. The prophet mocks the people, saying they ask, "When will the new moon be over so that we may sell grain; and the sabbath, so that we may offer wheat for sale?" (Amos 8:5). As we discussed in chapter 6, the fourth commandment set aside the Sabbath as a day of rest, a time for rejuvenation. It forbids work and all economic activity. But as Amos describes the people, they are impatient for the Sabbath to be over, willing the day to pass quickly so they can get back to their business of selling. Amos also echoes a theme that is common among the prophets, telling the people that God can't stand their worship because their religious rituals are empty (Amos 5:21); such worship is meaningless when they spend the rest of the week taking advantage of each other. And in Micah, the prophet asks rhetorically, "With what shall I come before the LORD, and bow myself before God on high? Shall I come before him with burnt offerings, with calves a year old?" (Micah 6:6). The point of these passages isn't that God doesn't care about worship or that the system of sacrifices described in the Hebrew Bible isn't a valid form of worship. It's that worship is meaningless unless it's connected with justice. The Bible often describes justice as what God wants from us. The passage from Amos leads into the resounding call, one of the favorites of Martin Luther King Jr., to "let justice roll down like waters, and righteousness like an ever-flowing stream" (Amos 5:24). Similarly, the passage in Micah concludes with an answer to the prophet's rhetorical question, with the famous statement of what God does, in fact, require of us: "To do justice, love kindness, and walk humbly with your God" (Micah 6:8).

The point is clear: Worship by itself means nothing. What matters is how we conduct our lives and how we bring this commitment to justice with us when we worship.

This emphasis continues in the New Testament as well. Although Jesus spoke occasionally about adultery and other moral issues (though he said nothing about homosexuality—apparently, this wasn't a concern for Jesus), he kept returning to his concern for justice. In Luke, Jesus launches his ministry by standing in the synagogue and reading a passage from Isaiah, announcing that "The Spirit of the Lord is upon me, because he has anointed me to bring good news to the poor. He has sent me to proclaim release to the captives and recovery of sight to the blind, to let the oppressed go free, to proclaim the year of the Lord's favor" (Luke 4:18–19). The "year of the Lord's favor" is a reference to Jubilee, mentioned briefly previously as a year when all debts are forgiven. In this brief statement, Jesus centers his mission entirely on the needs of the poor, the oppressed, and those who suffer from injustice.

We see from this that social justice is not an occasional preoccupation of the Bible or one that it happens to remember every once in a while. It is at the heart of the Bible's message: by some counts, over two thousand verses address matters of social justice.[3] When traditions focus on individual morality and leave out questions of how societies distribute resources, ensure access to legal protections, and oversee equitable relationships, they're missing a large part of the Bible's message.

THE MONSTER IN THE MIRROR

Like the prophets in the Hebrew Bible, horror can help us take a more careful look at what is oppressive and unjust in our world. Often, horror does so by providing an unforgettable vision of a world that's eerily similar to ours, so as to emphasize the ways that justice is missing.

A strong example of this is Jordan Peele's *Us* (2019), the follow-up to the writer-director's wildly successful and Oscar-winning *Get Out* (2017). *Us* is intellectually rich, deeply metaphorical, and mind-bendingly original, but along with this, it also has one more trick: it's scary as hell. My fourteen-year-old, a burgeoning horror fan, swears that *Us* is far and away the scariest movie they've ever seen. The two of us watched it together on a Saturday afternoon in our living room, sun streaming in from the window behind us.

While the plot defies easy summary, the simple hook is that the film is built on the scaffolding of home invasion horror, a staple of the genre since Humphrey Bogart's portrayal of a panicked hostage-taker in *The Desperate Hours* (1955). There's not much that's scarier than having a band of criminals burst into an innocent home, setting up a stand-off. But *Us* found something even more terrifying. In Jordan Peele's vision, the intruders who invade the Wilsons' home are the family's uncanny doppel-gängers, or mirror images. Peele imagines that each of us has a counterpart in a subterranean world, a group of people known as the Tethered. They are our unprivileged counterparts, people who suffer below so that we can live in luxury above.

Early in the film, a young Adelaide comes face to face with her doppelgänger in a funhouse mirror. Rather than seeing her own reflection, she is being confronted with her Tethered, and before long, we're left unsure as to who is the "original" and who is the Tethered copy. One of them is supposedly human, the other supposedly monstrous, but the distinction becomes blurry throughout the film. By the end, we're left wondering whether there's a distinction at all.

In the main events of the film, the unprivileged Tethered are rising from below ground to claim the privilege they believe should be theirs. Red, the only one of the Tethered who seems able to speak, describes her life as a tethered shadow to Adelaide: "And when the girl ate, her food was given to her warm and tasty. But when the shadow was hungry, she had to eat rabbit raw and bloody. On Christmas, the girl received wonderful toys; soft and cushy. But the shadow's toys were so sharp and cold they sliced through her fingers when she tried to play with them." For every good thing in life that Adelaide receives, Red receives the same thing, twisted into a horrible mockery. Instead of warm, nourishing food, the Tethered eat raw meat. And instead of exciting Christmas gifts, they receive toys that injure their bodies.

Us drives home the point that there is no just reason the world should be this way, why those above ground should prosper while the shadows below suffer. As Red further explains, "We're human too, you know. Eyes, teeth, hands, blood. Exactly like you." Nothing about this is just, and it places the viewers in an uncomfortable situation. While the Tethered are terrifying, with their wide, vacant eyes, malevolent grins, and menacing scissors, we also understand their claims to justice. They're demanding the privileges they've been denied in life through no fault of their own.

As an exploration of privilege, this scenario is brilliant. It takes questions of justice out of the abstract, and puts them squarely in human, individual terms. In the world Jordan Peele has constructed, one particular person suffers underground so that I can live my best life above. I am directly responsible for that person's misery. Like the prophets of the Hebrew Bible, the film shines a light on the injustices at the foundation of our current society. As Red asserts, the Tethered are "human too," just like us. And after we learn that Red and Adelaide switched places in childhood as a result of the prologue's chilling funhouse mirror scene, it becomes even more difficult to find anything to distinguish "them" from "us." The Tethered deserve a good life every bit as much as the people living above ground, making it harder for them to be discarded as monsters. While their methods are terrifying, their anger and frustration are driven by a call for justice.

It's not always Oscar-nominated prestige horror like *Us* that grapples with these problems. While *The Purge* (2013) is certainly a step or two below Jordan Peele's work in terms of quality, the film series raises difficult questions around justice, particularly in its second installment. Frequently, the films rely too heavily on jump-scares and people being saved at the last minute from a horrible fate by a character who appears out of nowhere, but it's hard to deny the ingenuity of the concept.

Set in a near-future America, society has elected to deal with its rising crime rate by instituting the annual holiday of the Purge, a night where laws are temporarily suspended and each citizen is on their own. The government's officially stated idea is that allowing citizens to release their pent-up anger and frustration on this night will keep them in line for the rest of the year—one night of terror and chaos in exchange for 364 days of peace and prosperity. From the very beginning, talking heads on news channels argue that the costs of the Purge are disproportionately borne by the poor, and we see this played out in graphic detail when an elderly man allows himself to be hacked apart by a wealthy group's machetes in exchange for a payment to his surviving family members after his death. In the world of *The Purge*, money can buy just about anything. For most people, it's enough to hunker down during the night in the hope of surviving to see the dawn. The first film follows the efforts of the Sandins, a wealthy family who have outfitted their suburban home with the best security system available. While it doesn't prove up to the task of fending off "purgers," at least it gives the family a fighting chance.

The struggles of the poor on Purge night, along with the motives of the government, are brought into clearer focus in the second installment, *The Purge: Anarchy* (2014). Instead of following a wealthy family in the suburbs, the sequel is centered on a low-income housing project. When the complex finds itself under attack, the residents gradually realize they aren't being randomly victimized by roving street gangs. Their assailants are government law enforcement agents, on a mission to clear out the low-income housing to make way for more profitable developments. The images of law enforcement officers striking at their own citizens are eerily prescient, foretelling the images we saw in the summer of 2020 when police tear-gassed peaceful protesters in Lafayette Square to prepare for a presidential photo op or pushed down an elderly peace activist in Buffalo, along with many other incidents.

What *The Purge: Anarchy* does so effectively is use this dystopian future to draw connections between government and corporate greed, power, and the ways in which that power can be brought to bear on vulnerable citizens. By the end of the film, it becomes clear that the "law and order" rhetoric of the film's politicians, as well as our own, is a thinly disguised message of class and racial domination. In the provocative (albeit heavy-handed!) third installment of the series, *The Purge: Election Year* (2016), a national election becomes a referendum on the Purge. The pro-Purge candidate uses "Keep America Great" as his campaign slogan, an echo of both Ronald Reagan's 1980 slogan ("Let's Make America Great Again") and, perhaps more obviously, Donald Trump's 2016 MAGA slogan. As the film unfolds, we learn that the pro-Purge party plans to use the night as a means of assassinating its political opponents. It lacks subtlety but is still a telling exploration of how the machinery of "law and order" works less to protect the average citizen than to preserve the interests of the powerful.

A further example of the sometimes barely concealed political ideology of horror films can be found in a place that might seem surprising at first glance: the ghost story. The key question always lies in the backstory of the ghost—what has made this spirit linger on? In some instances, it's as simple as that these spirits were evil in life, and they've continued being evil after death. Examples of this ghostly backstory include *The Conjuring*

(2013) and *Ouija* (2014). In both movies, the ghosts were murderous people in life, and their spirits want to stay on earth to keep doing evil things. That's simple enough. More interesting are films that offer a different backstory for ghostly beings, origins that make them more sympathetic, even if they are still terrifying.

In *The Woman in Black* (2012), a remote English village is haunted by the specter of a black-garbed woman; whenever someone sees her, a child close to them will soon die. But as solicitor Arthur Kipps (played by Daniel Radcliffe, still recognizable as Harry Potter beneath his beard) uncovers during his visit to the town, this apparition is the ghost of a woman who had been greatly wronged during her life. She had been an unwed mother whose sister took her child away from her and had her declared unfit. The bereft mother has been exacting revenge on the townsfolk for decades. A similar backstory is found in *Mama* (2013), in which a ghostly mother just wants to protect a pair of orphans, seeing them as replacements for the child who was taken from her in life. One might trace this trope (in film, at least) back to *The Uninvited* (1944), in which a house's hauntings turn out to be the result of a convoluted backstory involving a ghost whose child was stolen from her and who only wants her motherhood acknowledged.

While it might be possible to see these ghost stories as centering on the unresolved anger of these women, the real issue is one of justice. In both *The Woman in Black* and *Mama*, the ghost was a victim of patriarchal systems that controlled women's bodies and determined who was or was not fit to be a mother. *The Uninvited* also brings into play issues of race and class while telling the story of another woman whose child was taken from her because of her social situation. In her study of ghostly narratives, scholar Robin Roberts remarks that the figure of the female ghost "reveals the issues created by mothering in a patriarchal world."[4] These stories hammer home the injustice of the lived experiences of working-class mothers, who historically have had little voice or power. Like the Tethered of *Us*, the mothers of *The Woman in Black* and *Mama* are claiming their power and attempting to set things right in the only way they can.

IMAGINING NEW WORLDS

In both the biblical texts and the world of horror, we frequently see the injustices of our world held up for examination. Horror does this by imagining a slightly twisted reality in order to emphasize particular problems. When we imagine the Tethered, or a Purge night, or ghosts who wish to right patriarchal wrongs, we participate in a story world where these injustices are impossible to ignore. In these instances, horror serves as a twisted funhouse mirror, showing us our own reflection. It is obviously distorted—the existence of doppelgängers biding their time underground seems unlikely, and no politician has proposed instituting an annual Purge night, at least not yet. But in these very distortions, we see the uncomfortable truths that we wish we could continue sweeping under the rug. Often, the repressed monstrosity that returns to terrorize society is the direct consequence of conditions that human beings have created and continue to live in.

In this way, it's easy to see COVID-19 as a monster of our time, since it exposed the fault lines of injustice in society. As it became clear that social distancing would help keep people safe from the virus, society became divided into those who were privileged enough to work from home and those who were forced to keep going to their jobs. Again and again, "essential" seemed to be code for "expendable." The number of outbreaks in meatpacking facilities, along with those at other essential businesses such as Amazon warehouses and grocery stores, confirmed this terrible truth. Office workers and other white-collar professionals had the ability to lie low until the virus passed. Hourly workers got sent into the front lines.

The racial disparities of COVID-19 deaths were clear. Partially, this was because people of color were more likely to be employed in the essential jobs that required them to be in the workplace. But the pandemic also exposed a low-income housing crisis; while there was a brief pause in some foreclosures and evictions, many rental properties weren't governed by this moratorium, and the eviction ban was overruled by the Supreme Court. And in cities such as Flint and Detroit, which are both majority African American, utility companies shut off the water supply for some families who had fallen behind on their payments, even in the midst of a pandemic. (Though the relentless efforts of activists eventually resulted in a moratorium on water shutoffs in Michigan.)

In the way that the virus has disproportionately affected Americans of color, the realities of structural racism rise to the surface, with consequences that are stark and immediate. When workers are forced into unsafe conditions in meatpacking facilities, grocery stores, and Amazon warehouses because their contributions are deemed essential to our economy, it's impossible to deny that these jobs are deserving of a living wage and the kind of health protections that many Americans take for granted. The disparities also become starkly apparent in schools' distance learning plans, because the resources students can access vary hugely based on their zip codes. America may be a wealthy nation, but it continues to allow a huge number of its citizens to remain vulnerable for no other reason than protecting racial and economic privilege.

There are times when the biblical prophets present a vision of a dystopian future, like when they picture Jerusalem as a forlorn landscape straight out of a zombie apocalypse. The prophet Isaiah describes the coming destruction of Jerusalem and what will be left of the city: "But wild animals will lie down there, and its houses will be full of howling creatures; there ostriches will live, and there goat-demons will dance. Hyenas will cry in its towers and jackals in the pleasant palaces" (Isaiah 13:21–22). This desolate landscape, the prophet makes clear, will be the inevitable result of the people's continued pursuit of injustice. But the biblical prophets also imagine a new world where these injustices, disparities, and privileges no longer exist. For Isaiah, this will be a society where those who have no money can come, buy, and eat (Isaiah 55:1). Isaiah doesn't present us a roadmap for how to get there—the prophet's job is to give us the vision, not draw up a blueprint for its implementation. Our job is to give the vision flesh.

In contrast, horror rarely offers utopian visions of the future. (I say "rarely" because, while I can't think of an example, I'm open to the idea that I might be overlooking one.) Horror doesn't directly show us the world as it could someday be, but it implies that ideal through the cruel evisceration of the world as it is. When we see the Tethered confined to a miserable existence underground and realize that this is intended to represent the underside of our own world, we're called into the imaginative act of change. Both horror and religion expose injustices for what they are—the product of decisions people have made to protect their own privileges at the expense of others. When we see this, we should be moved into action, rebuilding the world according to a different image.

9

IS GOD GOOD?

PRECHAPTER VIEWING RECOMMENDATIONS

Frailty (Bill Paxton, 2001)
The Lighthouse (Robert Eggers, 2019)

Millions of Americans head to churches every Sunday—or log on to Zoom or Facebook Live—to gather as a community, sing songs, and hear an uplifting message. More often than not, that message boils down to a rather simple concept: Life may be hard, but God loves you. When you remember that God loves you, you can find the strength to endure all kinds of dangers, toils, and snares.

It's a powerful message, one that keeps believers coming back week after week. But it's only one part of our religious tradition, a particular aspect of our everyday experience of the divine.

Often, as we struggle through everyday life, it's easy to wonder if God really is good. These questions become particularly acute in times of need, like when a loved one is ill or we've lost someone we care about. We wonder if this is the same world that God called "good" in Genesis 1. When our lives are upended, placed on indefinite deferral, or even shattered, it's easy to wonder whether a compassionate God would allow this to happen.

It's a question that has frequently been asked by the biblical tradition, and by many theologians—both those deemed heretical by the church and those falling squarely within the range of orthodoxy. But it's also a question that has animated horror writers, usually in some way or another related to the Lovecraftian tradition of "cosmic horror." This point of overlap may be where horror's interest in religious questions becomes most clear. In the horror films I'll be exploring in this chapter, the horror isn't about the absence of God, although that can be a deeply rooted, visceral fear. (Ingmar Bergman, I'm looking at you here.) In films like *Frailty* and *The Lighthouse*, the fear is born of actually reaching God—and not liking what we find.

THE FEAR OF GOD

The Bible contains many instances where the people are commanded to love God. Perhaps the most famous is Deuteronomy 6:5: "You shall love the Lord your God with all your heart, and with all your soul, and with all your might," which Jesus quotes to a lawyer who asks him which commandment is the most important (Matthew 22:37; Mark 12:30; Luke 10:27). But that's not the only emotion the Bible asks believers to hold toward God. At least as prominent is fear.

Frequently, people in the Bible are described as fearing God, or told that they should fear. In the group of laws that are often called the Holiness Code (Leviticus 19–26), the fear of God is a repeated refrain. The people are told, "You shall not revile the deaf or put a stumbling block before the blind; you shall fear your God" (Leviticus 19:14). And later, "You shall not cheat one another, but you shall fear your God" (Leviticus 25:17). It's as if these specific commandments about being kind to the physically disadvantaged or being honest in business dealings are all summarized under the general command to fear God. When Abraham is traveling through a strange land and is afraid of what the inhabitants will do to him and his wife, he remarks, "There is no fear of God at all in this place, and they will kill me because of my wife" (Genesis 20:11), connecting the lack of a proper fear of God with a propensity toward violence. In a similar vein, Moses tells the Pharaoh of Egypt, "I know that you do not yet fear the Lord God" (Exodus 9:30). In these two passages, fearing God seems like the baseline description of what it means to be an ethical person. In the instructional book of Proverbs, the claim is straightforward: "The fear of the Lord is the beginning of knowledge" (Proverbs 1:7). Everything we can learn, it appears, stems from this foundation of fearing God.

Sometimes, what the Bible calls "fear" can mean something closer to what we might understand today as "awe" or "wonder." As the aforementioned quote from Proverbs demonstrates, fear of God is what spurs a person to learn and to become a better person. For Proverbs in particular, biblical scholar William Brown describes the fear of God as "the object of understanding and the basis of confidence; it is the source ('fountain') of a long and fruitful life, life in all its richness."[1] But in many other places, it's far less benign. In those passages, plain and simple, people are afraid in the face of an overwhelming presence that has the ability to do them serious harm. And in whose face they are utterly powerless.

In Exodus, the Israelites first experience the terrible power of God when they see what it can do to their Egyptian captors, including turning the Nile to blood, raining frogs down on the city, and, most terribly, killing the Egyptians' firstborn children. With this in their recent past, they're (at least sometimes!) smart enough to keep their distance from God during their wilderness wanderings. When they pause so that Moses can ascend Mount Sinai to receive the Ten Commandments from God, the people tremble in fear at the mountain's base, waiting for their leader to come back down. From their perspective, it looks like there is "a devouring fire on the top of the mountain," and the peak is covered in ominous clouds (Exodus 24:15–17). When Moses doesn't return as soon as they expected, they panic and build an idol, hoping that this will protect them from the terrifying God on the top of the mountain (Exodus 32). As portrayed in the Bible, God is one scary and unpredictable deity.

The idea of fearing God can make many contemporary religious people feel uncomfortable. A few years ago, I introduced the rock band I was leading at church to the song "The Search" by the sleepy Oregon alt-country band Dolorean. The song is a paraphrase of Job 28, ending with a chorus that affirms that "wisdom can be found in the fear of the Lord" and that true wisdom is about turning aside from evil. One of the band members expressed disquiet. "Could we change it to 'love' of the Lord?" she asked. We looked at the verse this line came from, Job 28:28, and found "fear of the Lord" written in bold ink. We decided to leave the line unchanged, even though it didn't give us the warm fuzzies.

The book of Amos, which we discussed in the last chapter, chastises people who are excited for God to come to earth and set things right. Amos has other ideas. "Why do you want the day of the Lord?" the prophet asks. "It is darkness, not light" (Amos 5:18). We have convinced ourselves that God's presence will be an occasion for joy, but it might be cause for wailing and lamentation. Or, as Philadelphia hip-hop collective The Roots put it, we may believe we want to see God, but when he actually shows up and we see him face to face, we "turn around and run." The reality of God might not be as consoling as we've been hoping.

Rudolf Otto, a German scholar of religion from the early twentieth century, worked with some of these ideas in his influential book *The Idea of the Holy*.[2] Otto was pushing back against the tendency of religious scholars of his time who saw the most enduring elements of religion as being the rational ones. Otto believed that Christians had spent so much time focusing on the rational characteristics of God that they were ignoring the nonrational ones, what he termed the "numinous." The numinous is the part of God that cannot be explained or understood rationally.

In Otto's reconstruction of the origins of religion, this nonrational element is what drew humanity to worship in the first place. He imagines one of our ancestors looking up at the stars and feeling completely inconsequential beneath the vast universe, deeply aware of their own vulnerability. This sense of fear in the face of the cosmos is the first step toward a sense of religion. Otto goes even further to suggest that most of our religious rituals and practices are grounded in this fear—not because holy fear inspires us to love God and want to worship, but because it provokes a harrowing sense of dread. Our rituals do a more or less thorough job of sublimating that dread. In other words, each of the rituals we perform—whether it's prayer, communion, or re-creating a manger scene on Christmas Eve—is about trying to convince ourselves that if we're respectful and humble enough before God, then the universe will be nice to us in return. It's a rather chilling conception of religion, and one that brings religion directly into conversation with horror. For Otto, our experience of horror is the foundation for all other religious expression. We're shaken by how insignificant we are against the immensity of the universe, and we participate in worship to lessen our panic.

SCRATCHING AT THE EDGE OF THE UNIVERSE

A concern with the numinous also undergirds much of cosmic horror literature, particularly the writings of H. P. Lovecraft. In the early twentieth century, Lovecraft wrote some sixty-odd short stories (some very odd), a trio of short novels, and a nonfiction essay called "Supernatural Horror in Literature." Most were published in the pulp magazine *Weird Tales* to a small but devoted readership; since his death in 1937, his influence has grown exponentially. Lovecraft moved horror from the staid ghost stories of M. R. James into tales of overwhelming existential dread, in which the very nature of the universe is called into question. His work was a major influence on later writers such as Stephen King and Neil Gaiman. But as we'll explore briefly in this chapter, his legacy is at least as problematic as it is influential.

In his essay "Supernatural Horror in Literature," Lovecraft identified the effect he was going for in his stories. He wanted the reader to be listening "as if for the beating of black wings or the scratching of outside shapes and entities on the known universe's utmost rim." Lovecraft believed that our perception of the world is limited to just an infinitesimally small piece of reality and that preserving this tiny perspective is the only way we're able to maintain a hold on our sanity. If we understood what the universe was truly like, our minds couldn't handle it. The human race's survival depends on our continued ignorance of the nature of reality.

The short story "From Beyond" (1934) demonstrates this proposition succinctly. As is often the case in Lovecraft stories, the first-person narrator has a close friend who is conducting some kind of mad experiment. It might have to do with reanimating corpses ("Herbert West—Reanimator," 1922), following a dark staircase leading down from a graveyard ("The Statement of Randolph Carter," 1920), or, perhaps most famously, an estate executor going over his late great-uncle's papers and finding that this relative learned about a sleeping God-monster that was due to wake up at any moment ("The Call of Cthulhu," 1928).

But in the stories, this friend frequently descends into madness, and the narrator serves as witness. In "From Beyond," scientist Crawford Tillinghast has created a machine that is unconvincingly described in pseudoscientific terms as creating a resonance wave that stimulates the pineal gland and allows people to perceive other dimensions. As Crawford starts up the machine, he's horrified to have a glimpse behind the curtain of reality. What we experience as empty air is actually filled with horrifying monsters, monsters that exist in another dimension that overlaps with ours. We usually can't see them because of the limits of our perception, but they surround us all the time. It's impossible for Crawford to live with the knowledge of this alternate dimension, and it drives him into madness.

This broad thematic structure is repeated over and over in Lovecraft's fiction. In the novella *At the Mountains of Madness* (1936), an Antarctic research team finds the remnants of an ancient civilization that predates even the dinosaurs. Some of this civilization's creatures seem to have been frozen for eons but are on the verge of waking up. The novella's narrator has written his tale as a warning to other would-be explorers to stay away from this snowy wasteland, "lest sleeping abnormalities wake to resurgent life, and blasphemously surviving nightmares squirm and splash out of their black lairs to newer and wider conquests." The only reason these creatures have allowed us to live, the narrator hypothesizes, is that we're too insignificant to merit their attention. But if we make our presence known, that could change in an instant.

At the Mountains of Madness and Lovecraft's other stories are markedly different from much of the horror genre due to the nature of the dangers their characters face. In most horror, we are afraid for the physical safety of the main characters; the primary action involves them being threatened by a monster who might eat them, slice them up, or subject them to any number of other terrible fates. Lovecraft's fiction features a very different kind of threat. Most often, the narrators observe events from a safely removed distance. They hardly ever see the monster, except in brief glimpses—most often, they only see the monstrous results that have been inflicted on a secondary character. There is no immediate threat to the narrators' bodies; instead, the threat lies in their understanding of the universe, and humans' place in it.

Lovecraft brings this motif to the surface in the well-known short story "The Call of Cthulhu," in which he most clearly lays out his ideas regarding the "Great Old Ones" who ruled the universe long before human history. The story begins with these famous lines: "The most merciful thing in the world, I think, is the inability of the human mind to correlate all its contents. We live on a placid island of ignorance in the midst of black seas of infinity, and it was not meant that we should voyage far." This could almost serve as Lovecraft's ars poetica, the thesis statement for all his fiction: We can only exist in the world because we completely and radically misunderstand its nature—and because we are too meaningless to draw much of the universe's attention.

In "The Call of Cthulhu," Lovecraft's narrator finds, in the research of unfortunate predecessors, clues about the nature of the Great Old Ones. They apparently came to earth from outer space millennia before humanity. They've been either dead or sleeping since then but are (perhaps) getting ready to wake up, an event that will lead to a horrifying cataclysm and the end of humanity as we know it. A small group of worshippers (usually associated with people of non-European descent, as will be discussed) have learned about these Great Old Ones through dreams and are preparing the way for their return. The story leaves the reader with the disconcerting sense that we're all living on borrowed time.

In this, as in so many of Lovecraft's stories, there's a hint that the universe contains far more reality than we can stand. But I'd be remiss to discuss Lovecraft, even in this brief overview, without mentioning the deep-seated racism that undergirded his worldview. It's not just a question of an occasional outdated use of language, although there's plenty of that too—the narrator's cat in "The Rats in the Wall" (1924) who has a deeply offensive racial slur as a name is only one egregious example. But even more than these surface elements, the structure of Lovecraft's world rests on white supremacy, a foundation that was explored brilliantly in the short-lived HBO series *Lovecraft Country* (2020). For Lovecraft, the prospect of racial mixing is terrifying. His understanding of a comfortable universe for (white) humanity to live in is hierarchical, and everyone's happy when we all stay in its prescribed lines. For him, the idea that Europeans would have descended from impure stock is a cosmic horror on par with the terrors Dr. Crawford witnessed in "From Beyond." In "Facts Concerning the Late Arthur Jermyn and His Family" (1921), the titular researcher delves into his ancestor's past explorations in Africa and sets himself on fire after learning that his bloodline includes a strange race of apes. It's an ugly, ugly worldview, which can't be easily extracted from the rest of Lovecraft's project. And it's a legacy that horror is still coming to terms with.

Lovecraft does leave us with a legacy of provocative, unsettling questions about our place in the universe, even if we sometimes have to imagine that he's talking about humanity as a whole rather than just people of European descent. These are questions with which Rudolf Otto would probably nod in agreement. In Lovecraft's universe, the monotheistic God that many of us worship is a fallacy; the universe is instead controlled by the malevolent Great Old Ones. Whether they're creators or just ancient beings is unclear, but they're certainly in charge of things now. Or at least they will be, whenever they decide to wake up.

THE GOD AT THE END OF THE ROAD

The horror movies I find most interesting are those that live right next door to Lovecraft. They don't necessarily posit a universe run by ancient cephalopods (although the 2016 thriller *The Void* is an awfully fun movie that does just that), but they offer a similar view of a world in which the guiding hand is not benevolent. In these movies, the horror isn't because God has abandoned us or never existed in the first place. In all of these works, the existence of a monotheistic God is a given. Instead, the question is about the nature of God. What if we were given a direct, revelatory insight into the character of God—and instead of finding compassion, we uncovered violence and disdain for humanity?

The disturbing 2001 film *Frailty*, directed by and starring the late Bill Paxton, explores these questions. The film starts with a young man named Fenton walking into a police station, claiming to have information about the serial killer known as the "God's Hand Killer." Most of the story is told via flashbacks to the small-town dust of rural Texas, 1979, as Fenton describes how this killer is connected to his childhood. Preteen Fenton seems like a pretty normal kid, but his younger brother, Adam, is already the kind of religious fanatic that you'd try to avoid at a party.

The two of them live alone with their dad; their mother died during childbirth. They're obviously struggling to make ends meet as a family, but they are getting by and genuinely seem to care for each other. But one evening, their father wakes them up to describe a revelation he has had—he believes he's been told by God that the end is near and that he and his family have been given the special task of hunting demons to cleanse the world. Soon, he shares with the boys a list of names he's been given of people he's supposed to kill, with the boys' help. The father sees these people as demons, and believes that God wants them dead. God even provides the father with the instrument of destruction: on his way home from work one day, a light from the heavens points him toward an ax that will serve as his divine weapon. The three of them—Fenton reluctantly, Adam with relish—begin capturing the people whose names are on their list, disposing of them in a creepy earthen cellar their father has dug for just this purpose.

We spend most of the movie thinking that Fenton is the only sane one in the family. Dad is clearly delusional, and there's something wrong with Adam; he dives into his role as righteous avenger with far too much zeal. But as the flashbacks give way to the present time, the man telling the story is revealed to be the grown-up Adam, not Fenton, as he has claimed. When Adam touches the police officer to whom he's been telling the story, a quick flash of memory reveals that this officer is not the upstanding man he is pretending to be and that his past misdeeds have put his name on Adam's new list. Most importantly, this reveals that Adam does, indeed, have some supernatural insight into the sins of his victims—with the implication that his dad did, too.

Viewers are left with a story in which access to the divine is real. Adam and his dad did have a mission from God—and this mission was to brutally murder those who had been marked as sinners. Not only does this God condone violent justice and use humans to carry it out, but God has no qualms about involving children in this plan. The film encapsulates the most violent, horrifying aspects of God (from both Testaments). This God doesn't bat an eye at killing the firstborn children of the

Egyptians, commanding the Israelites to wipe out entire civilizations of people, or consigning every sinner into a lake of fire in the final apocalypse. In *Frailty*, this bloody, wrathful God isn't tempered with love, compassion, or patience—there's nothing but vengeance. It's horrifying to think that God might be nothing more than this punishing force, that the being in charge of the universe is only concerned with handing out death.

Frailty presents one vision of a terrifying God; the 2019 film *The Lighthouse* presents another. It's a film profoundly out of time. Not only does it eschew color for black-and-white film stock, but it also stubbornly sticks to the almost square 1.19:1 frame ratio that was standard during the silent era rather than the oblong widescreen formats of today's big screen blockbusters and television series. There's minimal scoring or diegetic music of any type, the story unfolds in lengthy takes instead of rapid-fire editing, and almost all dialogue is delivered by two cast members. Like the director's previous film *The Witch* (discussed in chapter 5), *The Lighthouse* refuses to participate in current trends, and seems more intent on pushing audiences away from the box office than on drawing them in.

The film centers on two lighthouse keepers, grizzled veteran Thomas and apprentice Ephraim, sequestered together on an isolated island. Thomas is a harsh master, assigning Ephraim the menial tasks of keeping the lighthouse clean and running and then berating Ephraim for his inability to perform the tasks well or quickly enough. Through all of this, Thomas forbids Ephraim from entering the top of the lighthouse. It is not a space for apprentices. Stormy weather prevents them from being resupplied or relieved of their duties, and the two men gradually unravel and descend into drinking and arguing. Eventually, Ephraim murders Thomas and then heads to the top of the lighthouse against his mentor's instructions. He is blinded by whatever he sees there—a sight that is kept from the audience—and tumbles down the stairs to his death. The final shot is of Thomas lying on the beach, food for a particularly aggressive seagull.

The film presents the lighthouse as sacred space, and it shares with the priestly texts of the Hebrew Bible an awareness of the danger inherent in such spaces. Approaching God is dangerous, and the elaborate rituals of biblical books like Leviticus and Numbers are designed to keep people safe when coming into close contact with the divine. If rituals aren't done exactly right, they can lead to death. In Leviticus 10, Aaron's sons make an offering of incense and fire, but something about this fire was "unholy" (in the translation of the NRSV) or, more literally, just strange or even foreign. We don't know quite what they did wrong, but God sets them on fire as a punishment. Later in the biblical story, when King David is bringing the Ark of the Covenant into Jerusalem in a grand procession and it starts to wobble a bit, the priest Uzzah reaches his hand out to steady it. Rather than being rewarded for keeping the sacred object from falling to the ground, Uzzah is struck dead (2 Samuel 6:6–7).

What is this about? Highly skilled chefs train all their lives to be able to prepare the delicacy of puffer fish; when it's made right, it's one of the most delicious dishes there is. But the fish's organs are deadly poison, so if the chefs don't know what they're doing, the gourmet meal can lead to sickness or even death. Rituals in the Bible are a lot like this. They bring the people closer to God, but if they're not done right the results are catastrophic. The priests need to be exhaustively trained, deeply conscientious, and committed to perfection every time.

In *The Lighthouse*, Thomas plays the role of the high priest, with the care and keeping of the light being his daily ritual. Ephraim, in contrast, is the apprentice, learning the proper observances and developing the skills necessary to be able to approach the divine and live. But Ephraim feels drawn to the light in ways he can't quite understand—reaching the top of the lighthouse is a need that he can't shake, and it becomes even more intense as his isolation grows. It's akin to the desire for a genuine religious experience. Ephraim needs—with every fiber of his being—to reach the top of the lighthouse and experience the light for himself. He ends up being a moth drawn to the flame, and the light kills him. No matter how deep the need may be, this film suggests, we're not meant to get too close to the divine.

The dynamic that drives *Frailty* and *The Lighthouse* is fascinating; in both films, the characters yearn for an experience of God, and their quest is successful. But in both cases, what they find is horror. Of course, one of the most chilling aspects of *Frailty* is that Adam and his father unquestioningly accept this terror. "Who are we to judge God's will?" their father asks the boys. Adam, already immersed in religion (and possibly with a latent streak of sadism), is happy to go along with this. Fenton, in contrast, can't accept that murder is truly God's will. In *The*

Lighthouse, we aren't given insight into Ephraim's revelation—we don't know what he saw at the top of the lighthouse or what knowledge this gave him into the nature of the universe—but we know the encounter was fatal.

For myself, and I imagine for many of us, this articulates an important truth about our own religious experiences. At times, I can believe that God loves me. But when life gets harder, I start to wonder if God's paying attention or if there's more truth to the biblical portraits of a darker God than I'd like to admit. Maybe we suffer because there is no God, or maybe God exists but is out to get us. God doesn't seem to be doing anything good in the world, so I just hope that God's attention will be directed somewhere else, away from me.

For most believers, this isn't the sum total of our religious experience, but it's something that's real and palpable from time to time. It's also an aspect of the divine that every religion I'm aware of has explored in at least one way or another. It's real enough that our faith ancestors have acknowledged it for thousands of years.

When the message of our religion is reduced to "God loves you" and the world around us doesn't seem to reflect that love, we're too often left with a religion that doesn't match our experiences. Horror films like *Frailty* and *The Lighthouse* are well aware of this, realizing that it's preferable to give voice to this fear and trembling than to pretend it's not there. If our religious traditions don't acknowledge what is fearsome about the divine, then when we experience it we can feel like there's something wrong with us—like we're the only ones who feel anything but overwhelming love coming from God. While sometimes we might find comfort in being reminded of God's love, at other times it's important to acknowledge that we're frightened of the world and the universe and that it seems like the supernatural overseer in charge of it all might not be very nice.

Then we can gaze up at the stars, as Rudolf Otto imagined our ancestors once did, recognize how small we are, and be grateful for whatever piece of existence we have, for as long as we have it. And know that it's okay to be afraid, because sometimes the universe gives us good reason to be.

10

DOUBTING
THOMASES

Frankenstein (James Whale, 1931)
The Island of Lost Souls (Earl C. Kenton, 1932)
Sunshine (Danny Boyle, 2007)

In the self-help section of any bookstore, or in the world of personal improvement blogs, you can find all kinds of programs for overcoming doubt. When you doubt yourself, these tracts all say, you're wearing an anchor around your neck. You can't accomplish anything worthwhile in life. To be free of the shackles of doubt, you have to unlock the power of positive thinking and believe you can do anything, or some other similar string of clichés.

In the discourse of self-help, doubt is a negative, something to be overcome. It's the opposite of belief, a life-draining force that keeps us from achieving the things we want. Belief is strong. Doubt is weak. This dichotomy is easily transposed to religion, especially within contemporary Christianity. It's not hard to find step-by-step guides for the committed Christian to overcome doubt. When the belief/doubt dichotomy is understood this way, doubt is a stumbling block, something that tries to keep us away from God (and, in some traditions, away from our eternal reward in the afterlife—there's no room for doubters in heaven).

Except, what if that's not the whole story about doubt?

In this chapter, I want to make a positive case for doubt as an essential part of the life of faith and something that religious traditions should be encouraging. For me, doubt is not the opposite of belief—I would instead propose that the opposite of belief is apathy. Having doubts indicates that you care enough about these issues to wrestle with them and that the questions of religion and life matter too much for you to be satisfied with pat, oversimplified answers. Doubt is an active process, not a destination. When we doubt, we keep moving forward. When we doubt, we do not stop searching.

Horror has a long tradition of doubters, including some who make viewers sigh in frustration and others whom we admire. One common trope is the doubting patriarch who won't believe his family's stories of supernatural encounters even when a ghost slaps him in the face. And there's the clueless police officer who thinks the kids are just messing around when they tell tales of a killer at the camp or a meteorite from outer space. But there are also characters who don't believe that the boundaries we've placed around human experience are the whole story. It's these doubters that I want to raise a metaphorical glass to in this chapter.

We'll start by exploring the role of doubt for two prominent Western thinkers and then discuss a few places where doubt figures into the stories of the Bible before turning to the part doubt plays in horror movies. Throughout, I'll focus on the positive aspects of doubt, the ways in which it pushes us to clarify our belief systems and can generate new, imaginative ideas.

"I Doubt, Therefore I Am"

The seventeenth-century French philosopher René Descartes (1596–1650) started his "Discourse on Method" with the proposition that he would doubt everything, only moving forward when he could find something about that it was not possible to doubt.[1] This is how he came up with his famous formula "I think, therefore I am." For Descartes, doubt is the starting point from which you try to escape. It's the quicksand that our minds are stuck in—any philosophical journey requires pulling yourself up from doubt onto the solid ground of certainty.

But I've always been drawn more to the ideas of Søren Kierkegaard (1813–1855), the Danish philosopher who has often been considered a forerunner of the existentialist movements. For Kierkegaard, doubt isn't something you flee or shun. That's because knowledge doesn't happen as a straight-line journey, like a marathon that starts at doubt with the goal of getting to the finish line of knowledge as quickly as possible. In his work *Johannes Climacus* (Kierkegaard frequently wrote philosophical tracts from the perspective of fictional characters), Kierkegaard suggests: "Doubt is a higher form than any objective thinking, for it presupposes the latter but has something more, a third, which is interest or consciousness."[2] This whole work functions as an extended meditation on doubt; for Kierkegaard, doubt is what propels us, what keeps us searching. Someone who doubts is striving for a higher level of understanding. But knowledge itself is not the goal. The goal is the journey itself, which requires doubt.

If Descartes and Kierkegaard had ever attended a dinner party together (like in some strange *Bill and Ted's Excellent Adventure* kind of situation, where the centuries separating their lives didn't matter), I imagine that Descartes would have accused Kierkegaard of wandering around aimlessly. "We start from the same place of doubt," Descartes might have argued, "but I move toward certainty, while you spin in a useless circle." Then, I imagine Kierkegaard calmly responding, "I have the confidence to live in my doubts. You are so anxious to reach certainty that you try to leave the questions behind as soon as possible." I'm with Kierkegaard here. For me, the questions are what's most important. Doubt is what keeps us asking these questions.

More recently, the iconoclastic Buddhist teacher Stephen Batchelor has argued for the important role of doubt in the life of faith. Batchelor notes the Zen tradition that speaks of the necessity of "great faith, great doubt, and great courage."[3] It seems paradoxical, but Batchelor argues that this understands doubt as the quest to "keep alive the perplexity at the heart of our life, to acknowledge that fundamentally we do not know what is going on, to question whatever arises within us." He continues: "Faith is not equivalent to mere belief. Faith is the condition of ultimate confidence that we have the capacity to follow the path of doubt to its end." Similar to our discussion of faith in chapter 3, this view defines faith as trust—specifically, the ability to trust in your own doubt and follow the questions it raises rather than closing yourself off to the opportunities.

Of course, doubt doesn't always work that way. Sometimes doubt is an intellectually dishonest way for people to wave away information that doesn't fit their preconceived worldview. For example, while there are disagreements over the precise scope and some of the details about climate change, there's really no longer any legitimate reason to doubt the basic contours of the scientific consensus that it is real. I frequently struggle with my philosophical support for public education, even in the face of the evidence that charter schools can significantly increase the learning outcomes for students of color.[4]

When there's clear, decisive evidence in favor of one position, doubt is no longer an admirable position; it's willful ignorance. Not only should we keep asking ourselves questions about the things we believe, but we should keep asking questions about the things we doubt, to make sure we don't get ourselves sucked into a morass of misinformation. But with those caveats in mind, there's still plenty of room to explore good doubt. That kind of doubt might be difficult or painful, but it can stimulate fresh ways of thinking. That's the kind of doubt we'll be looking at in this chapter.

IN PRAISE OF DOUBTING THOMASES

In chapter 3, we discussed the power of faith, both in the Bible and in horror movies. When we think about what faith means, we often conceptualize an inner determination that can allow the person who wields it to move mountains (Matthew 16:20). But there are also places in the biblical text where the discourse surrounding faith is more complicated. One of those stories is found in the Gospel of Mark, when Jesus encounters a man whose son has been possessed by an evil spirit. The spirit "makes him unable to speak; and whenever it seizes him, it dashes him down; and he foams and grinds his teeth and becomes rigid," as his father describes him. In this and other stories of possession in the New Testament, many scholars have suggested that the real issue is either a form of mental illness or a condition such as epilepsy. In any case, Jesus's disciples are unable to help this boy, and Jesus is sure it's because of their lack of faith. But when the boy's father speaks to Jesus, he quickly disturbs this either-or idea of faith, as an object that someone either has or doesn't have.

Jesus claims that he will be able to perform this healing because of the faith he possesses. The boy's father responds, "I believe; help my unbelief!" (Mark 9:24). What a remarkable sentence. Is it simply an example of there being no atheists in the foxhole, so to speak, meaning that people who have previously been unbelievers suddenly find faith when they need it? I think there's something more interesting going on. The father is stating two contradictory things at the same time: He both believes and doesn't believe. This is an accurate picture of what doubt looks like—the mind wrestling between two possible options, weighing both but unable to settle on one over the other. Yet amid this wrestling, the doubter holds both belief and unbelief in tension at the same time. This man believes, and he doesn't believe. He knows he wants to believe, but he's not quite there yet.

While I've always been intrigued by this man, he's not the Bible's most famous doubter. That award has to go to Thomas, one of the disciples whose skepticism has given him a bad name for millennia. I have a great deal of sympathy for him. While Jesus gives him a hard time for how much it takes to get Thomas on the bandwagon, he's got an important part to play in the story.

Thomas gets a few brief mentions in the other Gospels, but it's only in the Gospel of John that he has any speaking parts or emerges as anything like an actual character. In one of Jesus's speeches to his disciples, Jesus tells them, "You know the way to the place where I am going." Thomas speaks up, "Lord, we do not know where you are going. How can we know the way?" This leads Jesus to his famous proclamation that he, himself, is the way (John 14:4–6). But the speech is propelled forward by Thomas's literal-minded question, the need for more information after Jesus's cryptic instructions to the disciples. In this Gospel account, Jesus is nudged toward his powerful self-description as "the way, the truth, and the light" because Thomas's doubt pressed him to clarify exactly what he meant. Without Thomas's doubt, there would have been no occasion for Jesus to continue his speech.

But of course, Thomas is most famous for his role near the end of the Gospel. When Jesus first appears to the disciples after his resurrection, Thomas isn't present. He first hears about it from the other disciples. But he's skeptical that someone could live again after death, and he's not going to accept it without concrete proof. "Unless I see the mark of the nails in his hands, and put my hand in his side, I will not believe," Thomas tells them. Thomas apparently holds fast to this assertion for the next week before Jesus appears to the disciples again.

When Jesus appears, he invites Thomas to touch his wounds. Thomas immediately recognizes that this is, in fact, Jesus, exclaiming, "My Lord and my God!" Jesus responds, in his customary laconic manner, "Have you believed because you have seen me? Blessed are those who have not seen and yet have come to believe" (John 20:25–27). Jesus begins by asking Thomas a simple question, which we readers know the answer to: Thomas's movement into belief is the result of having touched Jesus, of having experienced his wounds for himself. Maybe those who believe without needing the proof that Thomas required are blessed. But I'd like to think there are enough blessings for those of us who need a little more evidence—Jesus doesn't say the *only ones* who are blessed are those who believe without proof. Thomas gets a blessing, too. While the other disciples are Descartes, trying to reach certainty as quickly as possible, Thomas seems more like a Kierkegaard—stumbling sometimes, but asking the questions that move the narrative forward. Like the Zen tradition of great faith, great doubt, and great courage, Thomas dares to raise the questions that lead to greater understanding. Without his questions, we'd have fewer answers. And we'd be more likely to rush toward a faith that we didn't understand.

MAD SCIENTISTS' DOUBTS

The history of horror films is littered with the failed experiments of mad scientists, megalomaniacs who test the boundaries of human knowledge, consequences be damned. Perhaps the most famous of these is Dr. Frankenstein, a character best known from his manifestation of James Whale's 1931 film adaptation. In that movie, we see the mad scientist as a special kind of doubter—and one the horror genre respects, even if he (or, more frequently in recent history, she) brings a monster into the world through personal hubris. While the results of these mad scientists' experiments are seldom good, we also admire their determination, willingness to stand outside of what society deems acceptable, and single-minded risk-taking.

After successfully giving life to his patchwork doll of stolen body parts, Dr. Frankenstein (as portrayed with manic deliciousness by Colin Clive) famously proclaims, "Now I know what it feels like to be God!" This line was offensive enough that it was scrubbed from releases for many years.[5] It was also one of the lines that led to the inclusion of an audience-shaming prologue in which actor Edward Van Sloan (who plays the upstanding Dr. Waldman in the film), describes Dr. Frankenstein as "a man of science who sought to create a man after his own image without reckoning upon God." The hope was that local censor boards would be appeased by this refutation of Dr. Frankenstein's outburst. Indeed, the biblical allusion to Genesis 1:26–27, in which God creates humankind (both male and female) in God's own image, seems to reinforce Dr. Frankenstein's claim about playing God. Like God, Dr. Frankenstein created a new human. And like God, the scientist made this creation in his own image.

But the second half of the prologue's claim is odder; Van Sloan's statement that Dr. Frankenstein did this "without reckoning on God" seems to contradict the film itself. In the quote, we see that Dr. Frankenstein reckoned on God a great deal, so much that his relationship with God was practically his first thought after his experiment proved successful. For this researcher, the entire experiment is about unlocking the mysteries of life—which he equates with unlocking the mysteries of God. If he can understand the secrets of life, he believes, he can understand God.

Far from being a blasphemer, Dr. Frankenstein is a doubting Thomas, pushing for more understanding and restraining his belief until he's seen with his own eyes. Even more than that, he wants to use his doubts to expand humanity's understanding of what is possible—even if that takes us into realms usually reserved for God. By the end of the film, Dr. Frankenstein has, of course, repented of his mistakes, and manages to survive an attack by his creation. The film ends with him marrying his fiancée, a clear sign that he has been redeemed.

Usually, things don't work out quite that well for mad scientists. Even the most well-intentioned ones can find themselves transformed into a human-fly hybrid (*The Fly*, 1986) or impregnated by their own creation (*Splice*, 2009). The list of mad scientists' horrible ends is not a short one.

But even by those standards, the demise met by Dr. Moreau in the 1932 version of *Island of Lost Souls* is grisly. It's made even more powerful by the film's early date, which leads viewers to believe that what's being implied on the screen can't actually be happening, because there's no way it would have been allowed in 1932. Basically, his creations storm the laboratory, which they refer to as the "House of Pain," and use the doctor's own tools to vivisect him. Unsurprisingly, the film ran into all sorts of problems with censorship; even in the more permissive pre-code days, it was banned in fourteen states, and the British Board of Film Censors refused to certify it multiple times.[6] In the United Kingdom, it was finally released in 1958, in a heavily edited version. While its violence is certainly less graphic than what we're used to in horror films today, the disturbing undercurrents still leave me chilled every time I watch it.

Based on the H. G. Wells novel, Dr. Moreau has created his island empire through a series of experiments on animals, in which he has used all kinds of unsavory methods to try to help them evolve into humans. The island is populated with a horde of Moreau's experiments who have become self-aware enough to know that they're not quite people but not quite animals either.[7] Their self-awareness is most poignantly embodied in the Sayer of the Law (portrayed by Bela Lugosi), who leads these experiments through a liturgy: "What is the law?" he bellows, to which all the creations respond, "Not to spill blood!" Then he asks of the gathered creatures the all-important question, "Are we not men?" The question hangs in the air, without a clear answer.

But for me, the character of Dr. Moreau is still the driving force of the film. He's ego-maniacal, generally unconcerned with questions of morality, and has no qualms about inflicting large amounts of pain in the service of his pursuit of knowledge. Still, I find it hard to completely despise the smirking, wonderfully pretentious figure, particularly as Charles Laughton portrays him. He's evil, no question, but we admire his unwillingness to accept the limitations placed on him by society or by his own mind. He's driven by the same impetus that propels the Sayer of the Law and the creatures who lurk around Dr. Moreau's castle: they want to transcend their own nature. Many of us can find some degree of sympathy.

Of course, Moreau gets what's coming to him by the end of the film—his cruelty is too much to ignore and can't go unpunished. So while we wince at the sight of his creations descending on him with his own surgical tools, we don't shed too many tears for the mad doctor.

Even so, his character seems emblematic of the conflicting space that many mad scientists of horror embody. They have doubts about humanity's true place in the universe and wonder whether we haven't settled for too little. At heart, they're all doubting Thomases, prodding with questions that have the potential to move us all toward deeper understandings.

EXPERIENCING 3.1 PERCENT OF GOD

In the haunting 2007 Danny Boyle film *Sunshine* (the screenplay is by Alex Garland, who would later go on to write and direct the 2014 film *Ex Machina*), the sun is winding down, leaving the Earth cold, desolate, and without much hope for humanity. As a last-ditch effort, a group of astronauts aboard the prophetically named spaceship *Icarus II* has been tasked with delivering a massive nuclear bomb into the heart of the sun, hopefully kick-starting it and creating a new star within the dying star. They've got a plan that should allow them to return home after delivering the payload, but most of them seem to know that this is unlikely; in a realistic best-case scenario, they'll be able to restart the sun while sacrificing themselves in the process. This fatalistic reality is reinforced by the ship's name, recalling the figure from Greek mythology who flew too close to the sun and melted the wax on his homemade wings. We all want to transcend, Icarus reminds us, but flying too high is fatal.

While the film isn't short on sci-fi action sequences or horror scenes—it turns into a slasher film for about twenty minutes near the end—it's also heavy on metaphysical exploration. The sun represents the divine, the mysteries of the universe. The fact that it's dying seems like a clear connection with the current state of North America and Europe, which many observers have remarked are moving into postfaith societies. Our "sun," too, is fading. But in *Sunshine*, the crewmembers of the *Icarus II* know there is no more important mission than restarting the sun—in other words, reaching the divine.

Early in the film, we meet Searle, the ship's psychology officer, on the observation deck, soaking in the blinding sun rays with a pair of glasses. He asks the ship's computer how much of the sun he is currently experiencing; he is told that the current filter settings are allowing him to experience 2 percent of the sun. "Can you turn it up to 4 percent?" he asks. "Negative," the computer responds. "Four percent would be fatal." When he asks how much he would be able to withstand, the *Icarus* tells him that he could safely experience 3.1 percent of the sun's rays for a period of thirty seconds without permanent damage. Searle agrees and soaks up as much of the sunshine as he can. The look on his face is one of overwhelmed ecstasy. Searle has experienced a little more of the divine than he had thought possible and has lived to continue the search.

Searle's negative counterpart is introduced later in the film, when the crew hears a distress signal from the first ship named *Icarus*, long thought to have been lost. After a heated debate, the crew agrees to go after it in order to secure a second bomb for their mission. They find an abandoned ship, with the ashen remains of the former crew members in the observation deck. They apparently went above 3.1 percent. But as the *Icarus II* prepares to depart, its crew learn that they've got a stowaway from the derelict ship; the ship's captain, Captain Pinbacker, believes it is his divine duty to stop the *Icarus II*'s mission. Scorched by the sun from his years in space, Pinbacker says, "I've spent seven years talking to God." Pinbacker is a clear, physical reminder of the danger of proximity to the divine. In Exodus, after Moses meets God on top of Mount Sinai, he returns with a face that emanates light (Exodus 34:29–30). The result of Moses's meeting with God is inscribed on his face, and this reminder terrifies the people. Rather than being drawn closer to Moses because of his holy encounter, they run in fear. In a similar manner, Pinbacker has the result of his meeting with God written all over his body as well; instead of simply a face that shines, he is left with burned, disfigured skin, a warning of the dangers of being in the presence of the divine. (Unfortunately, disfigurement is often connected with fear in the world of horror films.)

Along with the damage to his body, Pinbacker has emerged from his years-long conversation with the divine with a clear understanding of what he believes his purpose to be. His transformation into a champion of certainty is a terrifying reminder of what humans can become when they leave doubt behind. Pinbacker claims to have learned that humanity's time is up and that the only proper course of action is to let the sun diminish of its own accord, making the earth an uninhabitable block of ice. Since he has been given access to the mind of God, he believes he is called to stop the *Icarus II*'s mission at all costs. Pinbacker's certainty is an illusion, a false conviction born of thinking his encounter with the divine has unlocked all of life's mysteries. His certainty actually represents a final ending, the ultimate stagnation. In contrast, the crew of the *Icarus* are moving forward, propelled by a doubt-fueled hope that what they know with certainty—that the sun is dying—is not the whole story. They need to keep exploring to learn more.

In my personal journey of faith, the closest I can come to answering any of the big questions of religion and spirituality lies in how I accept my doubts and my faith. If our faith is built on agreeing with a set of principles or propositions that we assert must be facts, then doubt can be a crippling feeling. It undermines any certainty about what facts are right and true. But if faith is grounded in a sense of trust, then our doubt and our faith can walk alongside each other just fine. They can be excellent traveling companions, and even conversation partners.

The question is whether doubt is spurring us on to new explorations, introducing us to thoughts, solutions, and ideas that we wouldn't have discovered otherwise—or leading us into intellectual malaise, where we allow our worldview to solidify at a fixed state, impenetrable to new knowledge. Good doubt is what propels us forward, in questions of science as well as in faith.

In *Sunshine*, we admire the crew of the *Icarus II* not only for their sacrificial devotion to saving humanity but also for their willingness to explore further boundaries and to keep launching themselves further toward the divine. In the Greek myth after which the ship is named, Icarus donned artificial wings in an effort to fly. While his immediate circumstances involved a desperate need to escape from the island of Crete, it is not difficult to read into this myth the human desire to transcend our limitations, soaring into realms that were not meant for us. Icarus wanted more than his lot had to offer, and he sought to expand his knowledge beyond the limits that had been set for him.

Of course, it doesn't end well. Icarus, drunk on his new-found freedom, flies too close to the sun, and the wax holding his wings together melts, causing him to plummet into the sea. Although the story is a cautionary tale, we admire his willingness to explore and to test the boundaries of human limitation. For many of us, our doubts are what continue to inspire this drive to move beyond whatever constitutes our known, comfortable world.

It's why I admire the unnamed man in the Gospels who believes and continues to doubt at the same time. And doubting Thomas, who's gotten such an unfair reputation from history. And the mad scientists like Frankenstein and Moreau, despite their streaks of hubris and cruelty. They keep striving and asking questions long past the point where many of us would have been satisfied.

Those questions are what keep me going. They're why I come back to church week after week, hungry for more answers. They're what keep me studying and wrestling with things I don't understand quite yet. Without a healthy sense of doubt, none of that would be possible.

I don't want to overcome my doubts. I want to continue living with them and letting them goad me on toward new ideas.

AFTERWORD

PRECHAPTER VIEWING RECOMMENDATIONS

The Toll (Michael Nader, 2020)

T hroughout my life, I've wrestled with two basic questions: why do I like horror so much? And why do so many other people feel the same way?

Researchers have posited a number of theories, including that the adrenaline rush provided by horror taps into a pleasurable part of our brains or that watching our worst fears play out on-screen—and surviving them at the end of the movie—is a way of overcoming them. There's obviously something to those ideas. But there's more going on, beneath the surface.

For me, the answer lies all the way back in my childhood, when I found myself moving beyond *Scooby-Doo* and into *Something Wicked This Way Comes* or looking for books that would stick with me longer than the Hardy Boys. Horror has the capacity to take the fears and anxieties of this world and put them together in a way that makes sense. Horror helps us assemble all the strange, disconnected pieces of our lives together into a story.

Surprisingly often, it's not all that different from the story we piece together through our spiritual practices.

The chapters in this book have explored many connections between horror and religion, but it seems to me that these connections have one thing in common: They're all rooted in the human capacity for imagination.

At its best, religion isn't a rigid system of rules but a way to expand the possibilities of what the world can mean, and what it means for us to live in the world. Our faith traditions have vast stores of wisdom—texts, practices, creeds—that help us see how our faith ancestors navigated these difficult questions and can guide us along the way.

And while characters in *Scream* and other postmodern horror films might joke about "the Rules" for surviving a horror film, the movies that have left an indelible impression on me aren't the ones that play slash-by-numbers like that. They're the ones that reflect the world around us. The reflection may seem dark or perhaps even appear as a funhouse mirror image, but the end result is that it either helps us think more clearly about the world as it is, or it imagines other ways of being that might be possible. These are films that ask questions about justice, and about hope, and about the ways that doubt can help us take the next step in our lives.

It might be hard to see how I find so much that's positive in the films we've explored that are fundamentally so bleak. So I wanted to end by looking at a film that doesn't skimp on the horror, but ends up in a place that's hopeful for the film's protagonist and its vision of the universe. Writer-director Michael

Nader's 2020 film *The Toll* finds a creepy Uber driver (Spencer) and his passenger (Cami) waylaid into an alternate dimension. As their car breaks down in a nighttime forest, they become stuck in an endless loop of past traumas and regrets. They learn that they have wandered into the domain of a figure known as the Toll Man, who only lets travelers go once they've paid his toll. Spencer and Cami soon learn that only one of them will be able to pass through alive.

The film smartly avoids overexplaining, but we gather that Cami has a painful background of an overbearing father and an abusive ex-husband. Furthermore, we find out that her initial suspicion of Spencer was well-founded—he reveals himself as a serial abductor, with Cami as his proposed next victim. But through the course of the film, Cami faces up to both the traumas of the past and the threat in the present, and Spencer ends up being the unfortunate one to pay the toll. While the film presents an unsettling universe in which the past can always return to haunt us, it's also a universe where we can overcome these traumas rather than being defined by them. And where it's the wicked who ultimately end up paying the toll. This encapsulates much of what this book has discussed: yes, horror introduces us to worlds that are dark and threatening, but it also shows us truths about the world that we're richer for having learned.

By its nature, horror is transgressive and mischievous. That makes it the perfect vehicle for challenging any assumptions we use when we are running on autopilot. It's a reminder that our religion should be like that too—challenging us and nudging us toward questions rather than keeping us comfortable with buttoned-down answers that haven't changed for centuries. We started this book with our first walk through the graveyard and into the sanctuary, raising the idea that there are things that lurk beneath the surface of religion. While it's less common for us to talk about fear on Sunday morning (at least in some churches), it's still the case that thinking through what our lives should look like involves asking uncomfortable questions about the monsters we see inside ourselves.

In the end, what lurks under the surface of horror? We've seen that it's the anxieties of a particular time and culture, whether that's the way American power is being used in wartime, societal fears surrounding the collapse or transformation of the patriarchal family, or the injustices that our economy is built upon. But horror also generates questions of how we keep moving forward when it seems like all hope is gone, what it means to have faith, and how we can come to a richer and more nuanced understanding of our place in the universe. As our understanding grows clearer, so does our capacity to create something meaningful out of the disparate pieces of our lives.

ACKNOWLEDGMENTS

There are few processes more solitary than writing; at the same time, the creation of most books requires a community. I count myself as deeply fortunate to have an incredible community of family, friends, scholars, thinkers, and horror fans who have contributed to the ideas of this book in ways too numerous to count. Without these relationships, this book would be greatly impoverished compared to the one you are holding in your hands.

My agent, Philip Turner, saw the potential of this project when I was still trying to figure out what I was doing and served as a tireless champion. Lil Copan and the rest of the staff at Broadleaf immediately understood the ideas I was trying to work with and continually pushed me to turn down the dial on my scholarly impulses and turn it up on my storytelling. My editor, Jana Riess, has been both kind and ruthless—the kind of editor all writers hope to be able to work with. And Ayanni Cooper, as the book's sensitivity reader, saved me from many embarrassing mistakes and oversights. Of course, the shortcomings that remain are the product of my own limitations.

The community at Ecumenical Theological Seminary has encouraged my rather odd scholarly passions and remained engaging and important conversation partners, even if over Zoom. I'm grateful to the faculty and staff who have helped me work through these ideas and to the many students over the years who have encouraged me to follow this academic muse. I'm also thankful for my faith community at First Presbyterian Church of Holt and its wise and caring pastors, Reverends Kirk Miller and Ben Rumbaugh.

Finally, I feel so fortunate to have found myself in a family that is more supportive of my work than I could ask for. My parents, Ed and Ellen, understood the importance of exploring ideas, even ones that can be uncomfortable. I continue to learn from my two children, Fenton and Reece, and look forward to many more horror movies together over the years. Finally, my wife, Kate Simon, has watched these movies with me (sometimes more than once), helped me wrestle with these ideas, and been a constant source of strength. While the words of this book were written while sitting alone at my laptop, the ideas contained within these pages are the product of countless conversations and relationships that have endured over many years. I give thanks for all of them.

NOTES

Introduction

1. I learned of the folktales referenced in this chapter from some of the essays included in *Storied and Supernatural Places: Studies in Spatial and Social Dimensions of Folklore and Saga*, ed. Ülo Valk and Daniel Sävborg (Helsinki: Finnish Literature Society, 2018), especially the contributions from John Lindow ("Nordic Legends of the Churchyard") and Kaarina Koski ("The Sacred and the Supernatural: Lutheran Church Buildings in Christian Practice and Finnish Folk Belief Tradition"). The book is published as open access, so it's available as a free download at https://library.oapen.org/handle/20.500.12657/29738.

2. Jason Bivins has a chapter on evangelical Hell Houses in his engaging book *Religion of Fear: The Politics of Horror in Conservative Evangelicalism* (New York: Oxford University Press, 2008).

3. The idea that cultural events can be found reflected in horror films has been explored by numerous scholars, including Adam Lowenstein's *Shocking Representation: Historical Trauma, National Cinema, and the Modern Horror Film* (New York: Columbia University Press, 2005). Also noteworthy is Victoria McCollum's *Post-9/11 Heartland Horror: Rural Horror Films in an*

Era of Urban Terrorism (New York: Routledge, 2016) and her edited volume *Make America Hate Again: Trump-Era Horror and the Politics of Fear* (New York: Routledge, 2019). My own essay on *The Witch* and *It Comes at Night* is included in this volume.

4. Robin Wood's essay has been reprinted numerous times; it's easily accessible as "An Introduction to the American Horror Film," in *Robin Wood on the Horror Film: Collected Essays and Reviews*, ed. Barry Keith Grant (Detroit, MI: Wayne State University Press, 2018), 73–110.

Chapter 1

1. Stephen Prince discusses this rule and notes some exceptions that seem to demonstrate the rather flexible manner in which it was applied in *Classical Film Violence: Designing and Regulating Brutality in Hollywood Cinema, 1930–1968* (New Brunswick, NJ: Rutgers University Press, 2003), 105–107. Prince summarizes: "While the editing 'rule' . . . may have had some force, it clearly was not binding" (107).

2. The film's DVD release played with this theme one final time. After watching the movie and returning to the main menu, the rear surround speaker makes a noise like a phone ringing. You've watched the film, and now in a moment of meta-play, you're getting your own call.

Chapter 2

1. The remarks on Psalm 23 from Clinton McCann come from his book *Great Psalms of the Bible* (Louisville, KY: Westminster John Knox Press, 2009), an excellent book that discusses eight psalms in language that is both accessible and informed by outstanding scholarship. When I teach the Psalms, I always

make sure to introduce my students to the work of Clinton McCann.

2. Wood, "Introduction to the American Horror Film," cited in chapter 1.

3. I first started thinking about the connection between *The Walking Dead* and theological ideas of hope from reading Kelly J. Murphy's essay "The End Is (Still) All Around: The Zombie and Contemporary Apocalyptic Thought," in the volume *Apocalypses in Context: Apocalyptic Currents through History*, ed. Kelly J. Murphy and Justin Jeffcoat Schedtler (Minneapolis: Fortress Press, 2016), 469–495.

4. Peele discusses his original ending in a *Collider* article by Matt Goldberg, "'Get Out': Darker Ending Revealed by Jordan Peele," *Collider*, March 3, 2017, https://collider.com/get-out-alternate-ending/.

5. If you're interested in a scholarly debate about the degree of apocalyptic fervor surrounding the turn of the millennium, see Richard Landes, "The Fear of an Apocalyptic Year 1000: Augustinian Historiography, Medieval and Modern," *Speculum* 75, no. 1 (2000): 97–145.

6. Part of this is due to Hal Lindsey's *The Late Great Planet Earth* (Grand Rapids, MI: Zondervan, 1970), coauthored with C. C. Carlson. When the end times didn't come about as Lindsey had predicted, he just updated the book with a new edition and sold millions more copies.

Chapter 3

1. Douglas E. Cowan discusses this scene in *Sacred Terror: Religion and Horror on the Silver Screen* (Waco, TX: Baylor University

Press, 2008), 84–90, as part of his conversation about "the religious imagination" in horror.

2. Marcus Borg wrote many books filled with engaging, accessible scholarship before his death in 2015. For his views on being both intellectually engaged and faithful, many readers start with *Meeting Jesus Again for the First Time: The Historical Jesus and the Heart of Contemporary Faith* (San Francisco: HarperOne, 1995). The specific discussion referenced here is from Borg's book *Reading the Bible Again for the First Time: Taking the Bible Seriously but not Literally* (San Francisco: HarperSanFrancisco, 2002).

3. Carol J. Clover, *Men, Women, and Chain Saws: Gender in the Modern Horror Film* (Princeton, NJ: Princeton University Press, 1992).

4. Translations of the Nag Hammadi library are found most conveniently in *The Nag Hammadi Scriptures: The Revised and Updated Translation of Sacred Gnostic Texts Complete in One Volume*, ed. Marvin W. Meyer (San Francisco: HarperOne, 2009). A scholarly yet readable introduction is Elaine Pagels, *The Gnostic Gospels* (New York: Vintage, 1989); Pagels is also the author of *Beyond Belief: The Secret Gospel of Thomas* (New York: Random House, 2003).

Chapter 4

1. For an introduction to censorship and codes in American film history, see Sheri Chinen Biesen, *Film Censorship: Regulating America's Screen* (New York: Columbia University Press/Wallflower, 2018).

2. See Ricard Gil, "An Empirical Investigation of the Paramount Antitrust Case," *Applied Economics* 42, no. 2 (2010): 171–183, for a succinct overview of this case.

3. Linda Kay Klein, *Pure: Inside the Evangelical Movement That Shamed a Generation of Young Women and How I Broke Free* (New York: Touchstone, 2018). Klein discusses purity balls and camps in an interview with Molly Longman, "Into the Dark *Pure*: Are Purity Retreats a Real Thing?" Refinery29.com, September 6, 2019, https://www.refinery29.com/en-us/2019/09/8360363/what-is-a-purity-retreat-virgin-into-the-dark-pure-hulu.

4. Freud discusses this in his 1919 essay "The Uncanny," which is often considered the fountainhead of modern horror scholarship (*The Uncanny*, trans. David McClintock [New York: Penguin Classics, 2003]).

Chapter 5

1. The 1972 film *Deliverance*, while more of an A-list drama than a straight-up horror film, is usually regarded as setting the pattern.

2. Jeffrey Jerome Cohen, "Monster Culture: Seven Theses," in *Monster Theory: Reading Culture*, ed. Jeffrey Jerome Cohen (Minneapolis: University of Minnesota Press, 1997), 3–25.

Chapter 6

1. The refrain is from Dylan Thomas's famous poem "Do Not Go Gentle into That Good Night," *Collected Poems* (New York: New Directions, 1953), 128.

Chapter 7

1. Bart Wilson, "Fair's Fair," *Atlantic*, January 25, 2009, https://www.theatlantic.com/business/archive/2009/01/fairs-fair/112/. Strikingly, the results change when the roles of proposer and responder are determined by some sort of contest, like which one of them scores higher on a quiz. When there's a rationale behind the proposer/responder hierarchy, the proposer feels free to claim a higher percentage of the cash, and the responder is more willing to go along with the arrangement.

2. Arlie Russell Hochschild, *Strangers in Their Own Land: Anger and Mourning on the American Right* (New York: New Press, 2016), 136–139.

3. David Hajdu, *The Ten-Cent Plague: The Great Comic-Book Scare and How It Changed America* (New York: Picador, 2008) is a great introduction to the horror comics of this period and the controversies surrounding them.

4. Robin Wood, "George Romero," in *Robin Wood on the Horror Film: Collected Essays and Reviews*, ed. Barry Keith Grant (Detroit, MI: Wayne State University Press, 2018), 373–375.

5. Laurie Goodstein, "After the Attacks: Finding Fault; Falwell's Finger-Pointing Inappropriate, Bush Says." *New York Times*, September 15, 2001, https://www.nytimes.com/2001/09/15/us/after-attacks-finding-fault-falwell-s-finger-pointing-inappropriate-bush-says.html.

Chapter 8

1. For a succinct summary of this history, see Bill Castanier, "EL REWIND: Historic East Lansing Battles over Racist Housing

Discrimination," May 3, 2015, https://eastlansinginfo.org/content/el-rewind-historic-east-lansing-battles-over-racist-housing-discrimination.

2. Ta-Nehisi Coates, "The Case for Reparations," *Atlantic*, June 2014, https://www.theatlantic.com/magazine/archive/2014/06/the-case-for-reparations/361631/. The essay has been reprinted in Coates's book *We Were Eight Years in Power: An American Tragedy* (New York: One World, 2017).

3. "A List of Some of the More Than 2000 Verses in Scripture on Poverty and Justice," *Sojourners*, n.d., https://sojo.net/list-some-more-2000verses-scripture-poverty-and-justice.

4. Robin Roberts, *Subversive Spirits: The Female Ghost in British and American Popular Culture* (Jackson: University Press of Mississippi, 2018), 41.

Chapter 9

1. William P. Brown, *Wisdom's Wonder: Character, Creation, and Crisis in the Bible's Wisdom Literature* (Grand Rapids, MI: Eerdmans, 2014), 37. For Brown, this attitude of wonder is what connects the Wisdom Tradition's focus on both the natural world and ethical relations between individuals.

2. Rudolf Otto, *The Idea of the Holy*, trans. John W. Harvey (New York: Oxford University Press, 1950), esp. 12–40.

Chapter 10

1. In Latin Descartes's famous phrase is *Cogito, ergo sum*. Descartes "Discourse on Method" is widely available in translation; the version I have read is John Cottingham's translation in René Descartes, *Selected Philosophical Writings* (Cambridge:

Cambridge University Press, 1988), 20–56. This piece was first published in 1637.

2. Søren Kierkegaard, *Philosophical Fragments/Johannes Climacus*, trans. Howard V. Hong and Edna H. Hong (Princeton, NJ: Princeton University Press, 1987), 170.

3. Stephen Batchelor, *The Faith to Doubt: Glimpses of Buddhist Uncertainty*, exp. ed. (Berkeley, CA: Counterpoint Press, 2015), 15.

4. "Urban Charter School Study Report on 41 Regions," Center for Research on Education Outcomes, Stanford University, 2015. A pdf of the report is available at https://www.heartland.org/publications-resources/publications/urban-charter-school-study-report-on-41-regions.

5. Sarah Bea Milner, "How Censorship Created Frankenstein's Most Iconic Line," *Screen Rant*, September 28, 2020, https://screenrant.com/frankenstein-1931-universal-classic-monster-censorship-iconic-its-alive-line/.

6. Jim Robertson, *The Hidden Cinema: British Film Censorship in Action 1913–1972* (New York: Routledge, 1989), 56–57.

7. It should also be noted that the film has uncomfortable connections with the nineteenth- and early twentieth-century pseudo-science of eugenics. As David A. Kirby notes, "The other characters constantly refer to the Beast People as 'natives' of the island, and their dark skin and hairy, hulking bodies are consistent with the stereotypical features eugenicists associated with 'inferior' African races" (Kirby, "The Devil in Our DNA: A Brief History of Eugenics in Science Fiction Films," *Literature and Medicine* 26, no. 1 [2007]: 83–108).